ENGINEERING YOUR MOOD

Feel Like The Person You Want To Be

BY:
LESLIE JUVIN-ACKER

Published by Leslie Inc.
P.O. Box 222
960 Postal Way
Vista, CA 92083

(760) 509-5449
www.leslieinc.org
officialleslieinc@gmail.com

ISBN: 9798833345634
Imprint: Independently published

Photo Credits: Justin Nunez http://www.justinnunez.com | @justinnunezstudio
Book Cover, Interior, and E-book Design by Amit Dey | amitdey2528@gmail.com

All rights reserved. No part of this book may be reproduced by any mechanical, photographic, or electronic process, or in the form of phonographic recording; nor may it be stored in a retrieval system, transmitted or otherwise be coped for public or private use, other than for 'fair use' as brief quotations embodied in articles and reviews, without prior written permission of the publisher.

The author of this book does not dispense medical advice or prescribe the use of any technique as a form of treatment for physical or medical problems without the advice of a physician, either directly or indirectly. The intent of the author is only to offer information of a general nature to help you in your quest for emotional and spiritual well-being. In the event you use any of the information in this book for yourself, which is your constitutional right, the author and the publisher assume no responsibility for your actions.

DEDICATION

I dedicate the message of this book to your intelligent power of being that is awaiting to express itself in innumerable forms. May you allow it to show you who you really are.

ACKNOWLEDGEMENTS

I acknowledge with the joy and oneness of being:

My family: Franck, Harper, and Donavon with whom I share in the delight of fun, silliness, and creativity in all its forms. For our honest communication, fidelity, and liberty of being. It's our world.

My community: For transparent, intimate, constructive conversation that leads to inspired action.

My clients and collaborators: For sponsoring my endeavors to awaken our true nature and collect our shared inheritance as part and parcel of the one-mind.

TABLE OF CONTENTS

The Illustrative Use of Words To Describe Your Mood. 1

Can You Let Yourself Be Happy?. 7

Get The Life You Want With The Correct Mood 13

If You Can Make A Decision, You Can Engineer Your Mood . . 15

Taste The Fruit of Your Mood. 19

The Origin of Your Mood 25

Using Words To Engineer A Mood 33

Appreciate Yourself. 37

Move From An Undesired Mood To A Desired Mood 41

Make The Sacrifice 45

A Self-Governing Body 49

A Mood Is A Thought In Motion 53

Enter Into A New Experience 57

How To Use The Mood List. 63

The Invisible Limb: Directing Your Attention 65

Dissolving Obstacles: The Barriers of Awareness 69

Entering Into Oneness. 73
Identifying False Self-Conceptions 77
Qualities of Mind That Form The Quality of Your World 87
Moods 93
A. 95
B. 112
C. 121
D. 135
E. 175
F. 183
G. 194
H. 197
I 203
J 221
K. 222
L. 223
M 228
N. 230
O. 232
P. 241
R. 251
S. 262
T. 285

U.	294
V.	306
W	308
Mood List A-Z	315
About Leslie Juvin-Acker	325

THE ILLUSTRATIVE USE OF WORDS TO DESCRIBE YOUR MOOD

All of my clients face the same conundrum:

A client enters into my mental experience. They use words from their own mental experience to describe their moods. They'll narrate with great detail their experiences with every kind of word that will accurately articulate their thoughts, their emotions, and behavior. They'll describe in great length other people's behavior, too, and how that other person managed to affect their mood.

Stories. We tell ourselves stories. Our stories usually don't make sense at all. That's why clients come to me to help them make sense of their stories. Their stories are usually not grounded in truth or based on sound reasoning.

One thing is true: *what* the client says to describe their experience is honest. They are really experiencing something that is bothering them. The experiences are real from a subjective, sensory standpoint. They're not lying about their experience when describing what's happening in their world. Their experiences are not fake. Their experiences are not "imaginary" in the sense that they're describing something that is not happening to them. It is happening in their experience. Their experiential inner world, to them, is very much real in a perceptual sense. They feel and experience the fruit of the assumptions that have conditioned their mind. Those thoughts may not be based on objective truths. They may be based upon false premises that create fruits of deceptive inner conditions, but the *sensory experience* the person has is very much real to them.

Take the example of a haunted carnival ride, the ghosts and zombies and boogeymen are not real. But they *evoke* real imaginary designs and sensory experiences. Or, a child afraid of the monster under the bed. The monster is not real, but the mental apparition and the corresponding fright *are* real to the child.

When a client is in a burdensome head space, their logical conclusions are based on false premises. They make up arguments against themselves and others. There is a good guy and a bad guy. There is them and some external force keeping them from being happy.

As logic and critical thinking shows us, an argument can be logical, but it doesn't necessarily have to be sound. The word *sound* means to have a premise based on an objective truth.

When you assume something to be true - for example, the statement that "I am a bad person," you have condemned yourself to the mood of self-condemnation. The paradigm by which you view life is skewed and inherently false. You do not really experience events and others as they are. Rather, you experience events and others as you see your own nature: bad.

Because of this false premise when you interact with other people, you assume that *they* believe you are bad, too. And, if they don't believe you're bad now, they'll eventually find out how bad you are. Because, by this logic, it's only a matter of time that you do something that bad people do. When that bad thing happens, you'll find yourself condemned by others. The condemnation proves just how bad you are. It's a sick, twisted form of logical reasoning. I've seen it too many times to count.

Often, clients don't know what they are feeling. They cannot articulate their moods. They tell me they don't know why they do the things they do. They say they can't make good choices to save their lives. They say they can't control their thoughts and that their thoughts either frighten them or make them sad or angry. Or worse, their thoughts make them want to give up.

If I ask a client who is stuck in an undesired mood to describe to me a solution state, they believe they are incapable of doing so because they are so conditioned to live in an undesired mood. They don't know *how* to think differently, they say. They just know that they usually feel bad. They don't know how they arrived at their undesired state, and don't know how to get out.

This is where self-talk comes into play. Your unseen, internal experience is formed by your self-talk. Self-talk is language based. The words of this language are formed by our deepest, innermost, secret feelings. Eventually, the mood in which you live habitually becomes so noisy that your self-talk becomes louder and stronger to the point that they override any conscious dialogue.

For example, a young mother told me that she always felt overwhelmed. That she would awaken in the early morning hours bombarded with swirling thoughts. She said waking up each day felt like starting all over again in an oppressive feeling that seemed to control her very existence. It was a bad Groundhog's day.

Knowing the opposite of overwhelmed, I asked her, "Do you know what quiet feels like?"

Dumbfounded, she responded, "I have no idea."

She said it was never quiet in her head. She felt as if her entire life experience was overwhelming, suffocating, and noisy.

Cognitively, we understand what quiet *is*. Psychologically, many of us do not know, from the depths of our being, what quiet *feels* like. The young mother could not articulate the sensations and thoughts of a quiet mood.

She could easily explain to me her overwhelmed state of mind. So I assigned to her the task of exploring for three days what being quiet *is*. I told her to imagine that I was an alien from another planet. As an alien, I had no idea what the concept of quiet meant, that it was her job to explain to me the concept of quietness. In order to do that, she had to experience quietness for herself. She had to observe and articulate quietness. From that place of quietness, she could not *be* - that is, experience - anything other than quiet.

The observer within us can only focus on one thing at a time. We think thousands of thoughts per day. The thoughts we focus on persistently with full mental concentration comprise the contents of our spoken words. The young mother's ability to concentrate on *quiet* for at least three minutes several times over the period of three days was her task.

Could she allow herself to enter into a psychological state of quietness?

Can you?

The ability to accurately describe an experience requires one to have lived it. When we habitually experience fear, stress, worry, tension, and conflict our self-talk reflects such psychological experiences. As a result, it can be a monumental effort to articulate with accuracy peace, expansion, flexibility, and confidence.

The hallmark of a good coach is the ability to guide a client from an undesired mood to a desired mood. The results that a client experiences as a consequence of entering into a desired mood is the additional benefit. Because, if a client is in a productive, or a peaceful, or a calm mood the results that flow from those moods are inevitable.

Therapies at all levels of the body-mind (mental, physical, and spiritual) are designed to move the mind from an undesired mood to a desired mood. If a patient does not feel better after a surgery, then the surgery was ineffective. If a patient does not experience a better mood because of the medication, then the medication is ineffective.

However, the fact is, the power is not in the procedure, the medication, or the therapy. The power is in the patient's capacity to shift from one mood to another. If the patient rigidly dwells in an undesired mood, the patient will take much longer to heal. On the contrary, if a patient is ready to stop feeling the way they feel and start feeling differently any therapy will work in a short time. The doctor, coach, or therapist must learn how to help the people who trust them to move from an undesired mood to a desired mood. Rapport is essential throughout this process.

The large part of my success as a coach stems from my ability to listen to a client's experiential narrative and successfully interpret their mood back to them. After the client feels like I have successfully accomplished this task because they finally feel validated and understood, they are ready to leave behind their mood in favor of a desired mood. They will then listen to me and allow me to employ their imagination by describing a new mood to them. Entrance into this new psychological state gives the client a new framework for experiencing life. When this occurs, the client no longer has to think and feel the old way. Rather, they can live life from a new internal experience. When the client feels different on the inside, life experiences appear different as a mirror to that change.

CAN YOU LET YOURSELF BE HAPPY?

There are millions of self-professed unhappy people in the world.

There are, equally, so many unhappy situations that we can find ourselves in.

But, are those situations really unhappy?

Or, do we exclude happiness from our experience and, as a result, make it unhappy?

Like the film *The Wizard of Oz* when happiness enters into our experience everything seems brighter, in full color, and expansive. When happiness, the substance and source of living, leaves our experience, everything suddenly feels repressive, narrow, and dim.

Is it possible to be happy when misfortune appears to befall us?

Is it possible that our feelings have very little to do with the events we witness and more to do with our own subjective, internal feelings of the experience?

As someone who specializes in emotional intelligence with hands-on, practical coaching experience I ask myself and my clients these questions daily.

Over the course of two years, I worked on a book about spiritual development centered around emotional intelligence. When I got over 76,000 words, I realized something important:

There is nothing outside of us that has the power to determine our mood, but we believe it to be so. There is nothing outside of us that makes decisions for us, determines what we get to experience, and the quality of our mood. This fundamental false assumption separates us from any hope of salvation from our erroneous thinking.

With this understanding, I trashed the entire book because I found a simpler, easier way to experience happiness without any type of protocol. It just requires focused attention and imagination.

But how can this be so?

People will say, "I've lost my home in a terrible storm, my husband died, my children were hurt, and I'm sick. I have every reason to be unhappy."

Some argue that being happy in situations where one should not be happy is a symptom of mental disorder.

When someone says to us, "My partner is leaving me and I have no money", we sympathize and say, "Oh, poor you. What a jerk! What a bad turn of luck!"

Why do we do that? Why do we, by default, play along? Instead of breaking the narrative and telling them the truth that they can instantaneously change how they feel about their circumstances, we assume the charade that they are subjugated to external conditions and that what they're experiencing is beyond their control.

I refuse to let anyone ruminate in an unhappy mood around me. Feel the way you feel, of course. You're perfectly entitled to experience life as you see fit. But have the courage to see yourself through. Recognize the feelings and then send them on their way. Withholding permission to be happy is a mentally and physically unhealthy way to be.

One day, I was lying next to my client, a successful business woman, in her guest bed - the only place she felt safe to express her deepest feelings - when she asked me a poignant question.

She asked, "Why wont I let myself go to (manage) my restaurant?"

I looked at her and instinctively replied, "The answer is in your question: You won't let yourself. You don't need a reason to not let yourself. You just won't let yourself. *Can* you just let yourself?"

Her eyes widened. Her face looked as if she was performing a thousand calculations.

After giving the question some thought, she could not find a legitimate factual reason explaining why she would not go to her restaurant. In fact, she profited well during the pandemic. She makes more money now than ever. Her business runs efficiently. There was no reason besides the fact that she simply did not give herself permission to get into her car and drive down the hill to her restaurant.

She simply made the decision to not go. She does according to her will.

As a coach, I could not make the decision for her. She had to decide for herself to return to her restaurant. As a strong-headed business woman, she also would not let anyone but herself make that decision for her. The truth is, she forgot that she alone unconsciously made the decision when she took on the mood that mentally and physically prevented her from returning to her restaurant.

After unconsciously having decided to not go to her restaurant, she tortured herself with self-condemnation. She concocted stories rationalizing why not going to her restaurant was so bad for herself and everyone. She made one painful decision after another without recognizing that her moods were determining her behavior.

I told my client that she unintentionally created a persona that thought, felt, and behaved in a way that she, her true self, abhorred. She admitted that she didn't like who she had become. She didn't like how she felt and was ready to turn a new leaf.

The funny thing is, we think life circumstances cause us to act a certain way. Contrarily the fact is, as this story of my client shows, nobody decides *what* we feel except us. We just don't realize that we *can* and *do* make all the decisions.

My client is not alone. We have all made decisions like this.

Think of the decisions you have made that have held yourself back.

Think of the times you simply would not let yourself be happy.

Think of all the stories you created justifying your decisions.

Or, the stories you concocted in regret of your decisions.

We rationalize our decisions every day.

These decisions and their associated rationale create the laws of our life. The laws we create determine what we *can* have, where we *can* go, who we *can* love, and what kind of career we *can* pursue.

We are all, in fact, self-governing.

We don't realize that we are self-governing. We unwittingly defer our decisions to the whims of other people, to economic conditions, to the memories of the past, and to the beliefs of those around us. We unwittingly, through passive mindedness, fall into a wide variety of moods. The good news is, we *can* choose our moods. We *can* decide which mood prevails over each of our days.

Instead, we imagine our way into disempowering moods that govern, by their nature, our thoughts, feelings, and actions. As a consequence, the experiences of our lives are built by the outpouring of our chosen moods. Our actions are determined by our moods. So, if we are to choose our actions, it is therefore essential to choose the right mood.

Alas! There is hope! If you can become conscious of an unwanted, undesirable mood, you can equally become conscious of a wanted, desirable mood. With practice, and eventually with great ease, you will exercise your ability to choose and change your mood within mere moments. Nobody will be able to take away your light ever again.

GET THE LIFE YOU WANT WITH THE CORRECT MOOD

Get the most out of life by getting the most out of your mental faculties.

When you feel good, you experience good, and you do good.

What you want may not be available in your current psychological state of thinking. So move into a new mood and you will find what is available to you there.

The thoughts, feelings, and actions associated with what you desire do not exist within an undesired mood.

You must enter into the mood that corresponds with what you desire.

There, in that chosen psychological state, the thoughts, feelings, and actions of the correct mood create the conditions for you to experience the fulfillment of your desires. As long as you are in the mood of aggravation, frustration, or fright, you cannot experience the fruits of another mood. You can only experience the fruits of the undesired mood.

Along this same vein, everything that appears unpredictable has an underlying pattern. Seemingly unexpected financial misfortunes run on a pattern. Chronic illnesses run on a pattern. Relationship conflicts run on a pattern. Why do the same problems keep happening? The problem is not *you*. The pattern is your habitual mood.

One can feel trapped in an undesired mood for what can be weeks, months, or years on end. This immobile feeling stems from an abstention of moving your attention to enter into a new, preferred mood. Abstention from attention direction creates mental boundaries that shackle the imagination. A mind abstaining and unwilling to expand farther than it can experience cannot expand beyond its present boundaries. As a consequence, one cannot do new things, have new things, or go to new places. The same old experiences come from the same old moods.

Moods shift in a seeming uncontrollable manner from one extreme to another. Sadness to anger. Depression to delirium. Fright to conflict. Our habitual moods can switch to the old familiar line up.

For example, someone might consistently switch between anguish, agitation, and confinement. A correction of core moods within the arrangement of one's mind can correct the trajectory of one's future life experiences.

Ask yourself some simple questions. Answer yourself truthfully.

What would you say are your habitual moods?

Which moods do you most often experience?

What results do you keep getting?

What events keep repeating?

Do you see a pattern between your moods and your results?

If you want to change your results, you have to change your mood.

You must select your moods so that they deliver the experience that you prefer.

IF YOU CAN MAKE A DECISION, YOU CAN ENGINEER YOUR MOOD

I experienced several panic attacks. I experienced a bout of postpartum depression and anxiety that lasted for months. I experienced the writhing pain of colitis. I almost suffocated to death by anaphylaxis. In these moments, I felt out of control of my experience.

The only thing that saved me from these psychological states was my decision making faculty. I could always make a decision no matter how terrible, helpless, and powerless I felt.

While lying in bed with postpartum depression, the thought of taking a shower felt the same as climbing Mount Everest without an oxygen tank. I didn't think I *could* do it. I had a conversation with myself about how I could possibly get out of the depression. I concluded with the directive to just make one decision at a time and *do* that. This time, it was to either stay in bed or take a shower.

I knew in my heart of hearts what was the better decision. I chose to take a shower despite as tormenting as going 20 feet from my bed to the tub felt psychologically.

I said to myself, "I'll just make one self-loving decision after another and I won't stop until I feel different."

In the years since, I have experienced intense periods of powerlessness, fright, and discomfort. I yearned to know why I felt the way I felt and began the journey of self-mastery. The contents of this book are a product of nine years of hands-on experience helping myself and many others to go from unwanted moods to desired moods.

The final tipping point for me was a year of loathing my intuitive abilities. I have a powerful imagination with the ability to see, hear, and feel the patterns of thought projected by other people. I believed that I *could not* stop empathing the mental patterns of others and it made me feel all sorts of ways I did not want. I decided that I could not go through life feeling the suffering of others. I no longer wanted to experience their experience of pain, remorse, and sadness. Rather, I wanted to always be a source of inspiration to help people shift out of unwanted moods. I just knew that continuing the way I was thinking before was unacceptable for me going forward.

It all changed when I got the idea to ask myself how I could stop feeling so influenced by the moods of others.

I heard the words, "I do sense a fortress of solitude around me."

At that moment, I could see myself in a large gray, stoney fortress, shielded by a wall of tall, thick trees. The leaves of the trees rattled gently in the wind. Centered in this fortress, I knew nobody - no person, nor figment of imagination - could find me. I was perfectly alone and serene in this fortress. My energy, my mind, and my body felt singular and quiet.

Then, I heard the phrase, "I do sense a sea of tranquility around me."

I saw myself on a private island on a bright and shiny day. The sea is quiet and still around me. I felt warm and calm.

This internal experience is no different than actually going to a real stone fortress or a real private island. I know this is true because I have literally experienced both environments during my lifetime.

The relief of experiencing the power of my own energy in imagination solved the problem.

Our experience *is* a product of our inner sensations. You can control your inner sensations through your decision making capacity. You can, by the function of harnessing your mental faculties, control your experience of life. If you can control what you think and sense with your feeling capabilities, you can control your behaviors. If then, by function, you can control your behaviors, you can direct yourself on the path of accomplishing your goals. It all begins by an active, decisive use of your attention.

I will teach you how to direct your attention and use your imagination to move from one mood to another. The results of moving from one mood to another will produce exceptional results. Because, if you can engineer your mood, you can engineer your finances, health, and relationships.

Try it yourself. Go anywhere you choose. Say, "I do sense..." and then complete the sentence.

TASTE THE FRUIT OF YOUR MOOD

*"A good tree cannot bring forth evil fruit,
neither can a corrupt tree bring forth good fruit."*

Matthew 7:18

Ask someone who is in an angry mood to calmly recite a poem. They can't.

By the function of a mood, one is only capable of expressing anger.

Ask someone full of rage to calm someone else in a comforting manner.

Without exiting the mood of rage, one can not enter the mood of comfort.

One mood can not produce the fruit of another mood.

Your mood is your psychological dwelling house. It is the vine from which the fruit of your mood blooms.

What you dwell on psychologically bears fruit. The fruit is the effect of amplifying a thought with your power of being. The effect is the external expression you call your experience.

For example, someone who is having an affair is not dwelling exclusively on their partner. Their mind, and consequently their psychological experience, is imaginatively elsewhere. Their actions, as a determined consequence of their predominant mood, reflect where they dwell psychologically.

Ask yourself, "Where do I dwell psychologically most of the time?"

What sorts of moods do you habitually feel?

If you feel stuck in a psychological state most of the time, then you are experiencing the consequence of a habitual mood.

One does not have to be an emotional intelligence expert to know that a person in a consistently angry or frustrated mood is highly unlikely to behave in a calm and focused manner.

However, most of us are completely unaware of the mood we consistently dwell in. We largely attribute our mood to life circumstances.

We claim that we are exasperated because of our children. We claim that we are angry because of the injustices in the world. We claim that we are sad because of the misfortunes of days gone by. We claim that we are frustrated because things don't work out our way.

In all of these statements, we attribute our mood to external events. We believe an external power determines what we think, feel, and do.

We assume that we cannot let ourselves be happy *because* of events outside of our control. We believe that we cannot allow ourselves to feel anything other than what circumstances *dictate* we should feel.

What does it mean to *let* ourselves? What does it mean to *allow* ourselves?

To let and allow is to free oneself to be something other than that we are conscious of presently being.

To be free is to exercise choice. To make a decision.

However, to feel incapable of exercising choice is based on the presumption that we are not free in any capacity; that someone else or some other force decides our present state of being for us.

The premise, therefore, creates the conclusion that we are incapable. Which then states we are powerless against all external and internal conditions. In short, because we live our lives believing that someone or something else controls our life experiences we are utterly incapable of changing our external environment let alone our internal emotional and mental environment.

Changing the unseen - that is, our internal, psychological environment - is essential to changing the visible, external environment of the world around us.

Simply, nobody can do anything about something without *first* deciding to do something about it. Without emotional resolve - that is, saying to ourselves "I don't accept this feeling anymore" - we cannot even begin to move our bodies and start acting differently.

That's why we see abuse survivors first making a personal, internal decision to get out of the situation. My mother was in a turbulent relationship for seventeen years to her first husband. Nothing that anybody could say would get her to stop participating in the turbulence until *she* felt resolved to do so.

How can you help another who is in a powerless mood to change how they think and feel, let alone what actions they take?

The answer is to assume the mood that they *do* have power and to always behave as if they are free to exercise that power.

In my work with high networth families I have witnessed a common malady. I work with professionally successful parents who have a child or children who experience depression, drug or alcohol addiction, dependency, or laziness. They go to great length and expense to have me help their child. Some of these parents believe that their child's behavior reflects poorly upon their own self-image or has something to say about their parenting choices.

The common way that these parents describe their children is "incapable."

One mother said, "I can't help but see my children as wounded little baby birds."

The first thing I do when teaching such parents is to correct their own mood regarding their child's growth. I consistently insist that their child is fine, doing well, and is progressing despite external conditions. The parent, for a while, makes the argument that, because of their child's past transgressions, they are incapable of achieving life-changing results in the future, let alone immediately.

I say to these parents that a person is not what they do, or what they think, or even how they feel. A person is capable of anything - gross atrocities as well as incredible achievement.

I ask frustrated parents, "If your adult child is capable of doing something you don't approve of, is it not also logical to suggest that your child is *also* capable of doing something you *do* approve of?"

When a parent decides that their child is *only* capable of making undesirable decisions - which is the common complaint of my clients - then they're only expecting undesirable results. The parent has written off their child as a never-do-well, destined to forever disappoint them. And, as a result, they can't help thinking about and dwelling on that disappointment. Then, when their child does something disappointing, their expectations are validated. They *"knew it all along"*. The feelings that they've dwelt on generate the mood of every future interaction. The mood the parent assumes determines the proceeding events.

I ask my clients to use their imagination and see their children as perfect, fine, and productive. When a parent is obsessed with every mistake their child has ever made, refusing to forgive and forget, it is not the child who is stuck but the parent's own mind. It is the parent herself who is *incapable* of change.

When a parent can shift their own imaginative machinations and therefore change their own mood, *how* they interact with their child changes. From this psychological standpoint, the parent is capable of changing their own thoughts, feelings, and behaviors in such a way that no matter what their child does they can relate to their child with oneness and understanding.

I have heard my clients say, "I raised them with standards." When their child does not live up to those standards, the condemnation and judgment are harsh. They do not know that their mood sets the standard by which they judge their child. As long as the parent is in an unfulfilled mood, nothing that their child does - not even a modicum of progress - will ever be enough.

That is why I emphatically implore all who read this book that if you want to help someone remember that they *can* decide how they feel and decide what they do. If one can make unhealthy decisions, they *can* make healthy decisions. Nothing, nobody, not even the seeming influence of drugs or alcohol can take away our decision making capacity. Ask an alcoholic which drink they want and they'll readily make a decision.

Remember that all conditions are consequences of decisions. We just forget the decisions that created those conditions. As a result, we falsely believe that we are trapped by a condition, a habit, or a psychological state.

Health conditions, financial conditions, living conditions, relationship conditions are all *consequences* of a persistent mood. We can and do choose our mood. Our persistent mood is our psychological home - it is the vine from which our life experiences bloom.

THE ORIGIN OF YOUR MOOD

"All ends run true to their origin"
- Neville Goddard

This chapter seeks to answer a few core questions.

Why do undesirable moods exist? Where do they come from?

Who are we? Where do we come from?

There are only two types of moods. Undesirable moods and desirable moods. You may call them truthful moods and false moods.

When we find ourselves in an undesirable mood, nothing good seems to happen. It's all bad. It's not fun. We feel trapped in undesirable moods; limited and powerless. Nothing seems to change in an undesirable mood. If things do change, they go from bad to worse.

An undesirable mood is a mood that shows us that we are subjugated by external events. An undesirable mood is the feeling of being trapped by the effects of our mental creations. This is called karma.

Grace, the realization that we can choose and create our experiences, automatically allows us to move from an undesirable mood to a desirable mood. When we ask ourselves, "What is the opposite mood of the very mood I find myself in?" We automatically, by force of deciding to be something other than this we are now aware of being, activate our imagination to find way from and out of the undesirable mood.

Undesirable moods are emanations of false assumptions. When we forget who we are, what we are connected to, and enter into a state of forgetfulness of the power we actually wield we believe - that is, latch on to - information that we assume is true based upon the evidence of our senses.

For example, someone tells us who we are, so we accept that they are right. We assume their external perception is an accurate description of who we really are on the inside. When people feel or act a certain way, we believe that some aspect of the world outside of them and us is the cause of their condition. This is known as the concept of duality or the dual mind. That is, a mind outside of our own controls our experience against our will.

A false assumption is a piece of information not based on truth. We assume that piece of information is a controlling, dominant idea that determines how we think, feel, and act.

If a person accepts the premise they are worthless, powerless, and insignificant, will they even be receptive to the idea that they can change their experience by simply changing their mood? This is the work of the therapist, the preacher, the coach, and the manager. Half of the work is convincing someone of the truth that they can do something about the way they feel. The other half is to get them to decide how they want to feel.

If we are convinced by lies, we cannot be open to the truth. The function of psychological pain in undesirable moods is a saving grace. Many live entire lives with lies controlling how they experience life. They forget who they are. They accept all sorts of lies.

Those lies eventually manifest in their body (the body is the solidified extension of the mind) as diseases, cancers, and chronic illnesses. So, they create and concoct stories of a power and force outside themselves that created the inner condition. There is suddenly a battle between good and evil. One can never hope to be free of this everlasting battle over the mind and soul. The outer condition determines the inner condition, but this is actually the opposite. Many, however, accept pain, suffering, and hurt as a normal part of their experience. One eventually succumbs to the lies if they do not desire to be free from the pain they feel or begin to wonder if it is even possible to live a pain free life.

Our lives are not supposed to be the search for truth. We are supposed to *live* the truth. *Remember* the truth. To *speak* it. And *feel* it.

Everyone from all walks of life can agree that it is noble and well to live the truth.

Unfortunately, there are many who believe a lie is a truth. Lies are proliferated as if they were the truth. All of it is to conform minds and control behavior for someone's personal desire for control of outer conditions. This, however, is a vain effort.

Some people say "The truth hurts."

These are the folks I like to ask, *Do you even know what the truth is? How would you know if it hurts?*

Ask yourself when was the last time the truth hurt you. A lie limits your mind. A truth expands your mind.

A lie is like high prison walls. You can't see beyond them. You can only see the confines of the lie. False premises limit our logic. They effectively put shackles on our minds.

Nobody is trying to deceive us. There is no grand conspiracy. People who spread lies are those who have first deceived themselves. If they have convinced themselves that their lie is the dominating law in their life, they too, by function, are convinced they are in a battle to defend their premises for how life operates and how we should be living it according to these rules.

So yes, there are people who spin lies and make a living off the exploitation of ignorance and fear. The only immunity from the moods of such individuals is to know the truth and to choose your own moods.

A mood is a reflection of our premises. Moods, emotions, thoughts, and feelings are all made of self-awareness. Consider all of these elements like the tools in an artist's workroom: paper, pens, markers, charcoal pencils, crayons, paint, and so forth. You, the artist, base your mood off of a premise. That premise might be, "I'm not making progress." From that assumption that is given expression by your awareness, you magnify it and amplify it, and give it form. You scribble, you draw, you fold paper, you crumble it up, you color and eventually you come up with a piece of art that expresses the mood of frustration.

Undesirable moods are not inherently bad, they're just not comfortable or desirable when misaligned with what we really desire.

The art of living is a creative process. How we create is through our moods. We create babies, buildings, playgrounds, art, diseases, conflicts, warfare, crisis, and all sorts of constructions and experiences based upon our moods. The rise and fall of nations depends on the rise and fall of a people's moods.

That is why we should never judge ourselves or others for the moods they find themselves in. We don't judge a baby for having a tantrum because they feel powerless to grasp the bottle on the high counter. I didn't judge myself at five years old when I was bereft at

Blockbuster when I did not understand why there was no video tape in the box on the shelf with the label "The Little Mermaid." My dad had to inform me that the video tape was safely behind the counter.

We are not here to judge ourselves or each other for our ignorance. We're here to experience ourselves and our creative expressions.

We are all using the elements and resources endowed by the origin of all experience. Some may call this God. Some may call this Source. Some call it the Universe. Some call it the fundamental laws of nature.

In the search for the most accurate word I could use to describe all of these and I found the word *origin*. I don't capitalize *origin* because it's not a person or a place beyond or outside of us. It animates you, me, all of us, and everything combined. It is the power that connects us and allows my distinct mind to know your distinct mind.

Further, I venture to posit that we are not individual souls that separated out of this origin. We're not lost. We're not cast out. We're not separated from each other or from the origin of all individuation. We're not trying to find our way back. We're not earning our way back.

My own observational experience has shown me that what we feel - this powerful presence and connection to all things - is our connection to origin. We're not individual souls that broke off. We're all a part of origin, the one mind, with individualized consciousness. We have been endowed with individualized self-awareness. We are part and parcel of everything that was, is, and will ever be.

This is why, as someone called a psychic medium, I can easily feel others feelings and emotions. It's why I can get glimpses into their memories or "past lives." It's why I can see their potential future, that is, the world they're building in their own individual minds.

I'm simply feeling into that connection to enter into your own unique mental arrangement - your established mood - and experiencing it for myself. I must admit that I stopped doing that for health reasons because I did not enjoy the feeling of dying, nausea, sadness, or loneliness that many of my clients have once felt. I had to find healthier, more enjoyable ways to validate the experiences of others without experiencing their suffering for myself.

Neville Goddard once said, "Rich man, poor man, beggarman, thief - these are not different minds, but different arrangements of the *same* mind."

I thought about this for years and years. Almost every day.

One day, as I simply sat with myself, I felt this gentle, calm energy inside of me. I felt my oneness with it. I realized that I don't have a *separate* soul. I am a part of the origin of my awareness and the origin is a part of me. That's why we can sense what animals are sensing. We can sense when danger is coming. Our intuition *is* merely a conscious awareness of this connection to origin.

This premise is fundamentally important because it sets the foundation for the creation of all future experiences. The logic goes: If we are part and parcel of origin and the origin contains all things beautiful, lovely, and good report then all of these positive experiences are a part of us and exist as potential within us.

We can become aware of this connection and go into origin through our imagination to generate desired moods. From the deliberate selection of our moods we can then build experiences that contain the objects, interactions, and behaviors we desire.

Alternatively, we can misuse our ability to create experiences. We do this ignorantly when we accept false premises as true and build our experiences based on false image making. False idols are merely images we believe have power to subjugate us to its will. These can be images of the devil, the enemy, the foreigner, the despot, the disease, the economy, etc. Any image or concept, or construct that we hold in our minds as wielding power to decide and consequently affect our psychological experiences is a false idol; a false god.

This is the one and only way we can create undesirable moods. This is the way we create mayhem, havoc, destruction, pain, and suffering in our lives.

It takes incredible mental self discipline to correct our thinking and to live only in truth. I do not recommend going on a crusade to free everyone from false thinking. I simply recommend to free yourself from false thinking and see how your personal interactions go from there.

Healing is simply moving from false thinking to truthful thinking. False mood to a truthful mood. I always say to my clients, "Nothing feels better than knowing you were wrong."

Become comfortable with acknowledging where you got things wrong. Feel comfortable with realizing the error of your ways so that you may enter into truthful thinking. Never judge yourself or others for experiencing the effects of their moods. Never judge yourself or others for ignorantly falling into a false mood. Simply ask the question, "What is the opposite of what I feel now?" And watch what happens.

USING WORDS TO ENGINEER A MOOD

Incantation comes from *incant*. Incant means *to sing*. To incant is to intone. To intone is to create a sound. A sound is a pattern that produces a structure unique to its own inherent qualities.

The sound of the word itself contains the emotional emanation of the mood we seek to express. Just by feeling a mood, we can create an entire dialogue that flows from it. Because the inherent quality of the mood shapes and forms the sounds and therefore words we form with our entire body and vocal chords.

The proper expression of a concept, when dwelled upon, invokes a mood. Every word spoken with our body contains a structure that is formed by a combination of our power and attention. We learn how to evoke moods with words. We use certain words to invoke a certain mood.

For example, political campaigners know how to engineer moods by the words they use in their political advertising. That's why internet ads and rage bait articles can successfully put people in a foul mood. By engineering moods, the writer of these ads can engineer behavior. By engineering behavior, the behavior by function of the mood operates the body that is possessed by it.

If a public is made to believe that there is a threat, then they can not, conversely, feel at ease. If a public is at ease and cannot be convinced of a threat, then they will remain acting at ease. If the public is convinced of a threat, they will begin to act as if there is a threat. Suspicion is aroused and an enemy is created.

A word, without feeling, has no power. That's why when a small child uses a vulgar word without understanding what it *means*, we find it amusing. But when a child uses a vulgar word with a full breadth of meaning, people feel the psychological impact of their words.

It is possible to speak without saying a word. Most communication occurs through body language. Research has shown that most communication doesn't occur with words at all. In fact, very little. Our bodies' physical movements and facial expressions communicate the inner dialogue of a mood.

Actors on a stage can communicate with us their character's mood without a single word. Children who are nonverbal can communicate their mood. Individuals with physical limitations can communicate their mood, as well.

Just as we can communicate a mood without words, we can pick up, understand, and articulate the mood of another. Regardless of culture, moods are universal.

Words help us bridge cultural gaps, but moods are ubiquitous and can be understood without knowing the culture.

There is an unspoken dialogue that generates thought, speech patterns, and behavior regardless of the language or culture. A mood cannot and does not lie. Words can be formulated to create deception, but moods never lie. Moods must be expressed by an individual one way or another. A mood, repressed long enough, can create disease through which one must confront their deeply held assumptions in order to release the hold the mood has upon their biological bodies.

A mood is very much a psychological experience as well as physical experience. The body, being a calcified extension of the unseen mind, reveals our deeply repressed moods. Diseases and illnesses show us the unspoken feelings of the mind.

All healing - whether surgical, medicinal, or contextual (stories, narratives, memories) - is healing of the mind. The biological body is as equally the mind as the spiritual consciousness.

Moods affect every system through which the mind experiences and expresses itself. To treat the body is to treat the spiritual consciousness. To treat the spiritual consciousness is to treat the body. Both are one and the same. The mood reverberates through all currents of experience.

It is essential to develop strong awareness of the non-verbal, physical expressions of a mood as well as its psychological emanations. The body talks. It's telling you something: your mood.

The better we can get at articulating with words our inner moods the better we can get at recognizing their impact on our lives. Doing so facilitates the process of shifting moods in an intentional way.

The process of engineering your mood, which is where you dwell psychologically, allows you to determine the types of experiences you want. Never again will anyone have the power to determine your mood once you know how to select and define your own experience. You don't have to speak English or even speak at all. You don't have to be very smart or well-read to create a desired mood. You just have to have the capacity to imagine and we all do.

You use your imagination every day, all the time. When someone tells you some bad news, you use your imagination to create what you think will be the outcome.

For example, your friend gets into a relationship with a person who you think is a bad influence. You imagine what you believe is the worst case scenario: your friend gets sucked into a toxic relationship, they lose all sense of self-identity, and your relationship crumbles because of the hold their partner has on their mind. You dwell on it every day and what you imagine determines your mood in the relationship with your friend. This is how we activate our imagination.

By activating your imagination on the *best case scenario* and constructing inner dialogue, images, and mental conceptions that reflect how you desire to feel you can effectively engineer your mood and thus your experiences.

It is helpful to learn to articulate your moods - even undesirable ones. If you find yourself in an undesirable mood, articulate your physical and psychological experience until you feel you have adequately recognized the mood. Give it a name. Decide for yourself never to enter back into that mood again and to create the opposite mood to experience instead.

Moods, false or truthful, reveal our conceptions of ourselves. Who we are is actually a power; a life giving force. If we limit what the power can do, we limit what *we* can do. We limit what we can create. Articulating our moods with words reveals to ourselves our unspoken limitations that limit our experiential possibilities. By releasing false assumptions that limit our creative potential, we open up infinite possibilities of good.

APPRECIATE YOURSELF

> *"For, as each soul is a part of the whole, individual in itself through the mind of the Creative Forces, it is thus - as a soul - a co-worker with or against that first cause or principle."*
>
> Edgar Cayce Reading 2113-1

Do you appreciate who you are?

Do you enjoy being in your own body?

Do you like being with yourself?

If the answer is no to any of these questions, then your task during the course of reading this book is to begin appreciating yourself.

The existence of any self-doubt, self-condemnation, self-judgment, or self-hatred will prevent you from moving out of an undesired mood. You must take it upon yourself to feel and experience your own wonderful, rejuvenating energy or life force. It is this life force - your true power and presence - that moves you and sustains you. This life force is the real you.

Some find it extremely challenging to sit quietly with themselves. The sheer power of their presence makes them feel uncomfortable.

It's just because they fear that power and what that power is capable of doing. So, we find ways to limit it or subdue it.

Some clients self-medicate with drugs or alcohol to avoid noticing that power. But, what they're really doing is just using that power to shift into a mood. There is no power in the drug beyond the power we, ourselves as that power, give it.

Learning to feel comfortable with oneself and in the awareness of your own power and presence is an essential skill for engineering your mood. Further, sitting comfortably in full awareness of our energy implies non-judgment; only observation. We are, at our very essence, a calm and powerful energy. We are, at our very essence, serene and peaceful. We are, at our very essence, still and quiet.

Most people don't know how to harness their power of being, but they do it every day. That is right: we employ our own personal power whether we know it or not.

We employ our personal power the moment we make a decision.

The powerful life force in us is the origin of all awareness and acts the moment we make a decision. Our decision making capacity is the application of our free will. Our decisions open the door for our true self to move from one mood to another. The moment we enter into a mood is the moment we change our lives. It's that simple.

If you can appreciate yourself, you can magnify your own personal power. You can intensify the experience of an active imagination and achieve results faster.

Self-loathing, on the other hand, felt intensely enough can accomplish the same task in an undesirable direction. So, it is vital to learn to enjoy being you and feel positive about your own existence.

One of the positive results born from the concepts in this book is that your perception of yourself is always improving. Your experience of the world is, part and parcel, an aspect of your own self-perception. As your self-perception improves, your world improves.

Sit quietly with yourself for 10 minutes. Simply notice the pulsation of your heart beat. Feel the rise and fall of your breath. Observe the radiating energy force in your body. Notice that energy force is circulating and pumping throughout your body to places that feel tight, achy, or swollen. Let go. By unclenching muscles you make way for that energy to flow. Take a deep breath and just experience your own energy.

All of your own experiences are experiences of your own mental arrangement. No, the actions of others are not a reflection of your own mental arrangement. There will be no victim blaming here.

How you psychologically *experience* their actions are a reflection of your *own* mental arrangement. How you *respond* to another's actions is a function of your *own* moods.

We cannot choose anothers' moods no more than we can choose their own psychological experiences. We can temporarily influence it, but we cannot decide for another where they dwell psychologically on a regular basis.

You can not choose how people behave or where they dwell because we all have free will. But, you can choose *if* you want to participate and *how* you want to participate by choosing your own mood. That is how we gravitate towards others and the experiences we find ourselves in. That is the means by which we are responsible for our own experiences.

So appreciate yourself and your own power. Return to yourself the power and authority over your moods. The moment we allow someone else to determine where we dwell psychologically is the moment we have subjugated the quality of our lives to an outside god. Own your power and use it for good.

By appreciating yourself, you set a healthy example for others. You encourage others to make their own decisions over their moods. You foster healthier relationships that are based on truth and liberty. You do not take responsibility for others who place themselves and dwell in undesirable moods. You recognize their capacity to enter into as well as exit undesirable moods. You see them not for the arrangement of their minds or their moods, but for the creative life force that they are and their connection to the origin of all personal experience.

You will realize that it is possible to co-exist with and love somebody who harms themselves with an undesirable mood. You will realize that it is possible to be happy, harmonious, and serene even when someone else is not. You will eventually be able to positively influence that person with a constructively employed imagination that sees them liberated from all limiting false assumptions.

Moods are temporary. Psychological experiences are temporary. The operant, animating power of moods is *you*. You, by function of your connection to the everlasting power that is the origin of being, are eternal. In the words of Swami Vivekananda, you are "an infinite dreamer dreaming finite dreams."

Appreciate your power. Value your power. Set your power free to go ahead of you and create for you the dreams that you decide are acceptable to you.

You are your power, one and the same.

MOVE FROM AN UNDESIRED MOOD TO A DESIRED MOOD

"An idea is salvation by imagination"
- Frank Lloyd Wright

The first place to start moving into a desired mood is the articulation of the present, undesired mood. It is easy to describe how bad we feel. Don't tell a story. Rather, describe *how* you feel and *what words* you think. Keep your observations scientific, rather than narrative.

You can say,

"I feel like…"
"I hear…"
"The thoughts I have are…"
"My body feels…"
"The images I see are…"

For example, in the mood of frustration, I felt:

- A tightness in my neck
- A clenching in my jaw

- Shortness of breath
- Blaming thoughts projected towards others
- Lack of blood circulation in my face, and, as a result, throbbing in my eyes, muscles around my head, and sinuses.
- Migraine.
- Emotionally, I felt unfocused, helpless, confused, and stuck.

The goal at the end of this observation process is to articulate with one singular word the *mood* you find yourself in. It is essential to be specific and accurate with the word to describe your mood. Once you have articulated your mood, you can then move into a new mood.

At this moment, ask yourself, "What is the opposite mood of frustration?"

When you ask yourself this question, decide to explore the opposite mood of frustration. When I explored this concept a list of experiences started to come alive in my imagination. I started to *think, emote, and perceive* the moment differently all because I decided to ask my attention to direct my power to *go* to this mood and enter into it.

When you enter into the mood opposite of frustration, your physical body - the extension of your mind into your own outer world - viscerally mimics your psychological experience. Your hormones, muscles, ganglions, and all other functioning parts of your body match the new chemical cocktail you've created in your brain. Your brain, thanks to your vagus nerve, communicates to your organs through the parasympathetic system. Your brain sends the message that you're no longer in the experience of frustration but rather the opposite of. Psychiatrically, you've given yourself a new biochemical experience.

This book identifies the most common moods. Undesired moods are named, but not described. It is your task to identify the undesired mood and articulate for yourself what mood you feel. The opposite, desired mood is described more in depth to give you a jump start in creating your own imaginative experience.

Even if you believe yourself to be of weak imagination or lacking in creativity, simply reading the desired mood and its description can help jump you into a positive state of mind. The best results come from actually experiencing and psychologically feeling the new mood from within yourself.

These words are in English. This technique can be applied in any language, but I still recommend that you use the closest description for your mood in your native tongue. There is a reason why Inuits have over 50 words to describe snow. A bad mood *is* a bad mood. However, the *kind* of mood you find yourself in differs in visceral and psychological quality from another. Rage is different from anger. Sadness is different from grief. Ache is different from sore. The difference may be slight, but this difference is consequential and requires accurate expression. Whether you speak sign language, French, or Chinese aim to accurately and specifically articulate your moods in order to find the opposite, desired mood.

False impressions observed by the awareness and accepted as prevailing law or authority over our lives limit experiences to a set of experiences assumed to be possible within the mood to which they correspond.

For example, one might believe that their economy does not value their work enough to enumerate it. They get the impression that society does not think what they do is worth paying large amounts of money for. Thus, it creates a mood of deficiency. It does not matter that what they do is actually valuable. The prevailing authority in this person's experience concludes that "enumeration" is impossible as long as "deficiency" is the prevailing mood. In short, one can't be paid lots of money for what they do as long as one believes that nobody is willing to highly compensate them for their work. The two experiences cannot exist simultaneously. You must, in effect, "choose which house to serve" (Matthew 24:14-15).

Accepting false impressions reveals a fundamental misplacement of our power and authority. False impressions are formed from false images observed in the realm of form. That is, the world you see with your eyes and hear with your eyes and define with your physical senses. Placing authority in external circumstances and conditions gives others power over your imagination and ultimately life. Placing authority in external conditions subjugates how you use your own personal power thereby limiting what you can experience in life. When someone or conditions created by others impress upon you, you are limited to what they think. In short, you operate your life by made up, false rules.

To free yourself of oppression, you must free your mind of false authorities. The task that is asked of you by this book is to free yourself of false impressions that direct your power into giving undesirable moods life.

You may not know what false impressions have authority over you, but you do know how you feel and this is where to start. If you can find a way to articulate how you feel, you'll be able to release your mind from false impressions that limit what you believe is possible for you.

MAKE THE SACRIFICE

We must strip ourselves of all disbelief. Disbelief is the act that denies the truth.

Truth is good. Truth is freedom.

Lay down all that is false on the altar of sacrifice and receive the blessings of a desirable mood.

Disbelief of the truth results in false thinking. All unloving actions, abuses, and exploitations are a result of our own denial of the truth. It's not "god" who is allowing bad things to happen. It's our own inability to accept and live the truth. It is our own misuse of power. By giving expression and form to false images with our inherent power, we give ourselves to undesirable experiences.

Forgiveness for sins simply means freeing ourselves from the moods that would have us act according to false thinking.

Sinning is the experience of denying the truth. Denial of the truth's existence creates a false experience. Denying truth is to hold a false assumption and consequently experience the effects of the assumption. The only sin is self-deception.

Through the very function of our imagination we create experiences with our own inherent power of being. This function is indifferent to whether we create undesirable moods or desirable moods. We, being the operator, set this function in motion the moment we affirm what we assume is true of this power. This power *is* you. This power is what you *are*.

People can create God/Origin/Universe/Source in a false image. We assume God is weak, fickle, vain, angry, condemning. We create this conception of God from a false conception of ourselves and humanity. God/Origin/Universe/Source *is* the power you are operating. Existence demonstrates operation. You can't *not* operate yourself. If your conception of God/Origin/Universe/Source is misunderstood then no wonder you've been getting inconsistent results. If your assumption of this power is one of being inconsistent, then that power you call God/Origin/Universe/Source reflects the image of inconsistency.

Your conception of this power, which is your true self, determines what this power and therefore, you, can do. If you limit the power/you, it functions on a limited basis. If you only provide it with limited imaginal acts, you get the same, tired experiences.

You, being one with this power, act according to your own conceptions.

Every experience mirrors what we assume is true about this power. This is how we create our own experience of suffering or salvation. The only intervening power to save us from our sins is the very power that we used *to sin*. The only difference is using it in truth.

Accept that the power in you can rejuvenate your physical body and it automatically begins the rejuvenation process.

Accept that the power in you can learn a new language and it automatically begins understanding it.

Children's minds are so capable of learning because there are very few limits they place on the power in them. Eventually, adults with limited understanding of the inherent power in all of us, create false stories and cultural myths about what is possible to experience and watch the potential of a child hit a wall. The wall is our own refusal to accept the truth of our own nature.

You can do what you believe the power in you can do. If you believe this power is God, then let God act through you. Be sure to remember that God is not separate from you, outside of you, or different from you. The moment you believe God is any of these qualities is the moment you limit yourself and place yourself at the mercy of an external mind's whims. God does not act contrary to you. God only shows you what you accept is true of you.

The Bible quotes Jesus as saying, "I and my Father are one." (John 10:30). If this is true of Jesus, this is true of you. It helps my clients when I say, "See yourself as God sees themselves. Then, remember you're God's child."

If, at any time in your life going forward, you find yourself in an undesirable mood, remember who can save you. You, through the conscious operation of the power of your being, can save yourself.

Athanasius of Alexandria said, "God became man so that man might become God."

This power of being limited itself into an individual experience to become conscious of itself and to know itself through others. We are one. Individually known to the One Mind.

The only thing to do is to correct one's assumptions. That is, what one accepts as true. Replace deception with truth. That is the only sacrifice we must make to live freely and abundantly.

A SELF-GOVERNING BODY

> *"Somewhere within this realm of imagination, there is a mood, a feeling of the wish fulfilled which, if appropriated, means success to you."*
>
> *– Neville Goddard*

Do the events of your experiences determine how you feel?

Do your current life conditions determine your outlook on the future?

Do the actions, attitudes, and choices of others determine your mood?

If the answer is yes to any of these questions, you are *not* self-governing.

Rather, you are governed by external conditions.

To be self-governing is to be aware of the unassailable, unchangeable power in you that is you. To give external events and conditions the ability to determine your mood is to avail yourself to subjugation. This is the one and only way we surrender control over our minds and consequently the direction of our lives.

Surrendering your own personal power to the external conditions of your present experiences gives others and the evidence of your physical senses authority over your ability to make your own determinations.

In other words, this authority - meaning, assumption that your external events are the ultimate truth of reality - supplies your logic with fundamentally unsound premises by which to base your judgment. Your conclusions - as a result of basing them off of false premises - may appear logical, but are ultimately false.

This is the process of self-deception and delusion from which we act incoherently, insane, confused, and disturbed. We can only think within the realm of false thinking long enough before the tree of false thinking bears its fruits. The fruits of false thinking are false moods. False moods influence behavior that are unakin to our true nature. So, we do things and feel things that are unlike ourselves. As a result, we live a life that is not really ours but as a consequence of external mental conditioning.

Notice when interactions or events of the day influence your mood. Notice how they take hold of your thinking. Notice how they lead you into a mental direction that creates discord within you. Any time you notice this inner conflict, you will become aware of the redirection of power.

Redirect your power.

Say to yourself, "I withdraw my personal power from all conditions that separate my attention from the origin of power. I center my attention to the origin of truth and from this place of being determine a truthful mood for myself."

Immediately after deciding for yourself that you will direct your power into the place which your attention has chosen, you will begin to notice a physiological effect. Your body will breathe easier, your muscles will start to relax, and your attention will feel able to think of other things. You will feel relief. What you have done is pardoned yourself from the condemnation of false assumptions.

False assumptions trap the mind into thinking only from the place of the falsehood.

There is no freedom in believing in anything but truth. Our attention becomes narrow in focus thereby limiting our perception to what is perceived outside of us.

There is no understanding to be found in experiences except to alert us to the assumptions that created them. All experiences offer evidence of our assumptions and invite us to either continue in their experience or to redirect our attention.

You may find yourself trapped in a situation that you feel is beyond your control.

Such as a minor in an abusive household, for example.

Remove your attention from the events around you. Redirect your attention to within the warm, energizing power within yourself and affirm to yourself that you give authority to that power to remove you from those conditions. Furthermore, give your inner power authority to neutralize all false assumptions that created these conditions by supplanting them with truth. Do not wait until you are the age of majority. Do it now in your mind. Trust that this power is presently acting in your mind to rearrange the conditions that placed you in the experience you have found yourself.

Deny all other power, authority, and control external to the power in you. And watch.

Patience is the ability to observe and recognize that the origin of truth is actively removing all illusions. Illusions are merely experiences that reflect a false thoughtform.

Remember that truth ultimately and always prevails over illusions.

There are millions of good experiences available to us, waiting for us to experience them. We can determine for ourselves the experiences we may discover. We do not have to wait for someone else to govern our lives and determine if we are worthy, ready, and able to experience goodness.

We are and can be self-governing through the simple direction of our attention which channels the flow of our creative, formative power of being.

A MOOD IS A THOUGHT IN MOTION

"So shall my word be that goeth forth out of my mouth: it shall not return unto me void, but it shall accomplish that which I please, and it shall prosper in the thing whereto I sent it."

- Isaiah 55:11

"*It's just a thought*" is an innocuous turn of phrase.

We say, "*It's just a thought*" when we have considered an image that comes to mind.

A thought can be a guidepost that takes life into an entirely new direction.

A thought can be a stop light that stops all forward momentum.

A thought can cause pandemonium if a terrifying image is accepted to be true by more than one thinker.

A thought, the moment it is accepted into our inner realm of imagination, can come to life. Thinking is creative action. A thought can be like a burning ember falling upon the fuel that is our latent power of being.

Quality of life is strictly determined by the quality of thoughts the mind sews into its own field of personal power. Our personal power is a fertile womb ready to implant upon its walls the fertilized egg of creative potential to replicate the instructions resultant of thought and power merging into one and bring forth a fully formed creation that is called experience.

A thought on its own is *just a thought*. It has no power even when seen on the screen of our inner imagination. We can dismiss thoughts. The moment a thought is given power, and therefore certain life, is when we impress upon a thought feeling from within our entire conscious realm of sensation.

We *feel* a thought's fullest expression from within ourselves with our ability to generate sensory experience in the inner realm of our unseen mind. In this hidden place of creation that exists solely within our own individual realm of awareness, we impregnate the faculties of expression - our imagination, the physical body's parasympathetic nervous system, reflexes, and thought mechanisms - to fulfill the instructions through collaborative construction.

Fertilized thoughts, one after the other, form the chain of life experiences. Within each and every experience is a conscious awareness of the quality of that thought. The quality of a thought includes the sensations, impulses, images, inner sounds, and perceptual lens of understanding. This explains why we "don't know what came over us" at any given point of experience when we feel submerged in a mood. We have long since forgotten that we alone have sown the seeds of experience in our own inner realm of creation. We do not remember that it was us who set the mood into motion.

A mood is a thought in motion.

A thought is a single, self-contained pattern that multiplies itself through the medium of mind.

A thought feeds upon imaginative sensations, strengthening in concentration and expanding until it is absorbed by the entire attention. This continues until it finally becomes born into experience; the merging of the unseen sensations of inner imaginings and the outer affirmation of fulfilled experience.

This is why we must persist in engineering the moods we desire to experience and to create the physical objects we seek to behold. Those who have convinced themselves of the reality of their thought act as if it is true. Their entire being acts in unison with this thought thereby perpetuating the pattern of the thought from within their mind, physical body, and behaviors. It is, in short, the essence of *fake it until you make it.* Pretend.

A thought, heard in the mind, is word. Spoken in acceptance gives it the permission to fulfill itself in you and through you.

Acceptance - the decision to enter into the perceptual reality of the word - moves you from where you presently are and into the fully expressed mood of the word.

Thoughts accepted are things that form the reasoning by which we base our actions.

A change of mood is a change of action.

A change of mood is a change of results.

A change of mood is a change of identity.

A change of identity is a change of destiny.

ENTER INTO A NEW EXPERIENCE

> *"That our old man is crucified with him, that the body of sin might be destroyed, that henceforth we should not serve sin."*
>
> *- Romans 6:6*

This chapter seeks to clarify the concept of the subconscious mind.

The phrase "subconscious mind" seems vague and uncertain. Many great teachers refer to the subconscious mind. However they go without providing stricter scrutiny to the meaning and scope of the word. And, there is a failure to instruct exactly *how* in practical, step-by-step application to employ the subconscious mind to create desired experiences.

There are many interpretations attempting to define what the subconscious mind is and how it operates to attain desired results.

The subconscious mind can be thought of as the mental arrangement of all assumptions that we accept to be the operating law and authority over our logic.

Our subconscious mind, or more narrowly defined as our mental arrangement, is our mental storehouse of assumptions that informs our decision making capacity and automatic habits. Simply, the subconscious mind is the totality of everything we accept is true.

For example, a person of one color grows up with the memorialized experiences of people of a different color being treated like animals. He then forms his assumptions from these external events. He observes people of a different color are somehow less than people of his color. Something inside of him - his connection to the origin of truth - makes him feel that something about these assumptions are wrong. Rather, he disregards this still, small voice because it goes against his self-conceptions and threatens the seeming power that this conception affords him over different colored people. He denies the truth and suppresses the logic that flows from it. He builds up arguments to substantiate his claim that different colored people are inferior or flawed and thus deserve inhumane, unequal treatment. Others who share this view agree and together they build a horrific dystopia built upon false premises through their actions.

It isn't until someone uses the authority from which he bases his logic against him, forming an opinion that something about his own identity is distasteful and thus deserving of inhumane treatment. He then meets the fullest expression of the mood he entered into. At this point, he seeks salvation from this inner conflict. The only solution of which is to change the law - that is, the fundamental authority by which he bases his own behavior - to a higher truth that everyone regardless of color or identity is deserving of humane, equal treatment.

The subconscious mind is then met with conscious consideration. He decides to replace the false rules with new rules. He says, "I'll never do that again," or "That's not how we do things anymore." And from this authoritative law, he then moves forward in life in a new way that assures desired outcomes.

Life plays out every single mood until we come to recognize the original thought from which it sprang. We then symbolically "meet ourselves". What goes around does come around in a simple sense. We always reap what we sow without fail.

How long it takes for us to meet our karma, or original *act* of acceptance as it is more accurately translated from Sanskrit, is how long it takes for us to realize the error of our thinking.

There is no punishment, only logical consequences of our assumptions. The only way to save ourselves is to release the false assumption from the subconscious arrangement of our mind in order to create a new world. In doing so, we create a higher, truthful concept of ourselves.

We must exit an undesired mood and enter into a desired mood. Entering into a new experience requires us to surrender to the authority of that experience's truth. This is a function of letting go of all opposing assumptions that would prevent our desired mood from realizing itself through us.

We must effectively let go of the old psychological version of ourselves in favor of a new psychological version of ourselves. This is the process of letting the old man die: the old psychological version of ourselves is destroyed in correlation to the death of the false assumption that no longer has primacy over our logic.

Forget the past errors of thinking and take on a new mind. A new mind creates a new life. We can not think the way we used to think if we are to experience a new lifestyle. We must think as the person we want to be in order to have the life that the new version of ourselves is capable of fulfilling.

Enter into your own mental arrangement by simply feeling with your imaginal senses. You implant the inner mind by thinking feelingly of a thought. The process of thinking feelingly generates the mood by which the thought expands and is given full expression in our imagination.

The thought is successfully implanted when you can not think the old ways anymore. You couldn't even think of it if you tried. The old thoughts and events feel like a distant memory. Emotional attachment no longer exists to memories or thoughts. You observe memories or events with a detached perspective. Eventually, you will know that the inner mind is successfully implanted when you have "visions" or "glimpses" into the "future". You are simply seeing the pattern of the desired mood expressing itself through your very power of being.

The vision or preview of the events feels real, as if you were there, and as if it really happened. This is the evidence of the everlasting *now*. It's all happening now. The events that unfold as a reflection of these moods happen sequentially as we continue through each experience. That's what gives you the sensation of time.

You can feel in these visions a sense of timing like "spring" or "next week". You may feel a sense of direction like, "I was in Greece and you were in New York." You may have a sense of dimension where you can move your hands around your body and point to where things are around you even though they exist only in your imagination for the present moment. You may have an emotional experience such as, "And, we were so happy together." You may also have a sense of conditions such as, "I was no longer working there."

These are no more supernatural events than they are natural consequences of the moods you have chosen to experience. You see things before they happen only because you are attuned to the pattern contained within the mood you have chosen.

It is a natural ability to be in the present moment and experience in your imagination events as though they were as real as the present. This is simply moving the attention from present events to upcoming events.

You have the right to see for yourself the logical consequences of your moods *before* you experience them in outer expression. This is why people called psychics can see potential events in your "future". They can access the shared connection to the origin of all knowing and get a glimpse of your mental arrangement. From there, they too can see where things are headed for you. You can change them if you do not like them, too. Everyone has this ability.

To implant the inner mind is to think feelingly of any thought which then generates expression through you. To ignore an unimpressed thought renders the seed of creation inert. To surrender yourself to a new thought kills the potency of the old thought. And, when you find yourself implanted by a false thought and have surrendered your power to an external authority, simply implant your inner mind with the mood that would be your salvation. Die to the old man and be born again.

HOW TO USE THE MOOD LIST

"...be purposeful in self. These as we find are the attitudes: What would the body do with itself if healed? Promise that - believe it - do it!"

Edgar Cayce Reading 2685-1

As you have learned, a mood is an embodiment of thoughts, feelings, and emotions. A mood is a psychological home wherein your attention dwells.

The latter part of this book contains thoughts distilled into a single word. The single word is a seed that contains the instructions for the expression of a mood that, when implanted into the inner sensory experience of the imagination, will come alive through conscious experience.

You may dwell upon the single words themselves and allow your own creative faculties to perform the work of giving form and expression to the word. Or, you may direct your attention to each sentence contained within the word and allow your imagination to be directed into a curated experience that will activate your inner senses. Reading the paragraphs that follow each word is like reading a fiction novel in which you are transported in imagination to a different realm of thought. Dwell on a thought until it becomes real in your imagination, or inner mind.

Each mood can be thought of as a new contract with yourself. This contract creates the operating instructions with which you will conduct your mental activity. It sets the premises by which you will establish your logic.

Read the mood you desire to embody whenever you feel ready to receive the new instructions. You may read them before you go to bed and allow those thoughts to be the final thoughts of your day to dwell upon. This is highly recommended and helps to set forth the desirable events of your upcoming day.

Read the mood before you take a nap. Or, when you're feeling very relaxed.

Reading a mood is also very helpful when you feel caught in an undesirable mood. Read it over and over until you feel your mind shifting into the desirable mood.

As soon as you recognize that you're in an undesirable mood, you can pick up this book and read a mood - any mood - to begin activating your imagination towards the fulfillment of a desirable mood. Stretch your imagination when reading the words and phrases of this book. Just as you would enter into the scene of a fiction story, enter into the scene created by each mood. The scene is experienced in your imagination, fulfilled when you sense with your inner feelings, and expressed when you behave in the corresponding manner.

You can train your mind to enter into beautiful places in your imagination. You can discipline yourself to think and speak gently of yourself and others. You can learn to behave in life affirming ways.

Reference this book over and over until you can create for yourself new inner experiences. You may discover new moods that are not listed in this book.

THE INVISIBLE LIMB: DIRECTING YOUR ATTENTION

Imagine that you have an invisible limb. This limb can stretch to the ends of the earth. Your invisible limb can go to any place, be with any person, and touch anything formed and unformed.

Imagine this invisible limb is like a hand on a long, invisible arm. Close your eyes. Send this hand to someone you love and touch them on the shoulder. Observe what you sense when you have done this. Take an inventory of the impressions you receive. Then, when you are done, remove your invisible hand away from them and bring it back into your body.

This is the process of sending your attention forth into creation. It brings back to you the knowledge of the person, object, or place that you felt after.

You can do this to bring objects into your experience. This also works with items that you know you need, but you are not sure of what specific kind. For example, you know you need a mattress, but you are not yet certain what brand or what place to get it from. This can also be accomplished for locating the right job, school, or community that best corresponds with your present life goals.

Using the "invisible limb" is not to be used on objects that belong to other people that they are not yet ready to relinquish. This is not done to "possess" something. Rather, using your "invisible limb" (directing your attention) can be used to bring forth things you, your family, or loved ones require to accomplish a specific good act.

Step 1: Become aware of your own presence by breathing into yourself and touching with your imaginal senses the inside of your physical body and outside of the body in the surrounding area.

Step 2: Create an invisible hand with your imagination, feeling the hand stretching forth from your abdomen or head. You could even make the invisible hand the size of your entire body.

Step 3: Move the hand around with your mind. Make it bigger and make it smaller.

Step 4: Stretch forth your hand to feel after the object you intend to "grab". Feel after the object: Where is it? What does it feel like? Can you describe the qualities of the object?

Step 5: Imagine grabbing the energy imprint of the object with your invisible hand and pulling it back towards you and then allowing it to enter into your own distinct presence.

Once these steps are complete, allow the object to enter into your experience in the best way for it to enter. Go on about your affairs, knowing that you did the job of feeling after the object, person, or experience.

Everyone does this process of moving their attention all of the time. It could be with finding something to eat for dinner. You say, for example, "I don't know what I want to eat, but I know it's light, fluffy, and savory." Before you know it, you've gotten the idea for the perfect meal and immediately go into action to fulfill your imaginal act.

You can do this for a special person that you'd like to bring into your life. You can say, "The right person for me accepts me for who I am, likes dogs, and loves to travel." As you send your invisible hand out, you sense after this special person.

Where your attention goes, your feeling grows. Once your attention fully absorbs your imaginal design you enter into oneness with it in your experience. Your mood indicates the accomplishment of *what* your attention has become one with.

Instead of feeling hopeless, impotent, and stuck, stretch forth your invisible hand to feel after any solution. Move your attention and focus it on what you feel in your imagination. Absorb anything with your attention. This process actively engages your attention and constructs with your imaginal sensations a new experience. You have officially and successfully entered into a new mood of your choosing.

DISSOLVING OBSTACLES: THE BARRIERS OF AWARENESS

The acceptance of obstacles causes the most delay in achieving results and prevention of experiencing peace during the creative process of living.

The acceptance of obstacles is the assumption that one cannot see the path of fulfillment. Obstacles prevent the ability to orient the attention towards solutions, answers, means, and ways out of an undesirable moods. An obstacle is the seeming barrier that surrounds the prison of an undesirable mood.

Go back to the earliest time in your life where you first believed there was no way out of an undesirable situation. It could be when your parents were fighting, or when you lost someone dear to you, or when you got hurt in a significant way. Something *bad* happened *to* you and it felt like there was no way to escape how you felt about the circumstances, conditions, or choices that created the suffering you felt deeply within yourself.

Can you feel the wall that confined you within that mood? We have all languished inside the prison of an undesirable mood whether through unrelenting feelings, images, or thoughts. Or, through a combination of all such sensory impressions. When you take a deeper look, it seems that the obstacles are tight, rigid, hard, impenetrable, and larger than you.

You do have the ability to uncreate the obstacles surrounding an undesirable mood and set yourself free from limited awareness. There are no obstacles, really. Only limited awareness. What you must do is to break free from the habit of limited focus that makes you *feel* trapped in situations, events, and conditions that you don't like; to break your attention free from the types of thoughts that would have you feeling paralyzed, helpless, and powerless.

There will never be an end to false thinking as long as people turn away from and deny the truth. You will see people in your life expose themselves to negative, false thinking. You will witness all sorts of absurdities and atrocities committed by such foolish thinking. You do not have to succumb to any of it. And, you can still continue living truthfully, peacefully, and serenely even if others do not.

This may seem to contradict the truth that we are all one and connected. The idea is that if one suffers, we all suffer. This does not have to be so. We all live in our own, individual state of consciousness. The *power* that animates *what* we are conscious of being *is* that *connection* we *all* share. It is possible for one to suffer and another to be liberated in the same time and space. Go to any party, business, or home and you will see that is so. What tips the scales of *whether a false or truthful* assumption dominates the moods of the people in a shared time and space is *how many* people believe it.

To believe is to accept. To accept is to take in and use the idea as a premise by which to base your actions. Think of an acting workshop, for example. An acting coach tells half the actors on the stage to pretend they just got dumped from someone they really loved. The acting coach tells the other half of the actors to pretend that they just escaped an abusive relationship. What would be the basic premise by which the actors would base their moods and therefore actions? Factually speaking, both sets of actors experienced a relationship split. There were two people who were at one point in an intimate relationship who are now separated and emotionally distant. What are the psychological conditions that make the cases so distinct?

If you are able to understand this example of distinction, you can see that people handle similar situations differently. How people experience similar situations is all a matter of mood. The mood is based upon what ideas you base your choices on.

The habit I urge to impress upon you is to investigate the quality and source of what you give your attention to and what thought you accept as the primary source of mental and physical action. Inquire, using a process of questioning, as to whether or not the thought is true or false. You have the right and the power to either accept or deny it as an operative thought by which to base your decisions and actions. You do not have to accept anything that is not true.

The presentation of obstacles in our minds is a symptom of limited focus. Ask yourself, "What am I not aware of?" And, "What truth is available to me that will expand my awareness and therefore dissolve all obstacles related to the conditions I'm presently experiencing?"

These fundamental questions will help you dissolve the barriers of false moods and expand your awareness to greater truths. As a result, you'll get the answers to your questions. You'll create a door where there are only walls. You'll create a passageway where there was only the waters of deceptive illusions.

When you turn your awareness to the origin of all truth available to you, truth always makes a way where there seems to be no way. So turn away from external conditions, for there are no answers *out there* to be found. Turn within to dissolve the obstacles in your mind

- the false belief that you cannot see your path of fulfillment - and make a habit of feeling for the truth within you that illuminates the connection you have with the one-mind. There, all the answers can be found. There, you are free.

ENTERING INTO ONENESS

To be who you want to be, enter into the desired mood (thoughts and feelings) and focus on the thoughts and feelings with your attention until your attention merges the desired mood into your power of being. You successfully merged your imaginal design with your reality. You merged your private world with your public world; your inner world with your outer world.

Everything good you would like to bring into your experience already exists in your inner world - the world to which we all possess a connection. Heaven can meet Earth by calling forth into your world what you design in imagination.

There is only one mind. You are part and parcel of one-mind. You are a distinct self-aware part of the one mind and origin of all awareness and truth. Each person that you know is a distinct, self-aware part of the one-mind. In each of us, we share a connection to the creative intelligence that is available to all.

You use your attention to bring your own individual power of being into oneness with your imaginal designs. You form your moods by becoming one with the thoughts and feelings that would compose that mood.

Just as you can use your imagination to construct beautiful images, you can use your imagination to construct false images. The one-mind does not create false images. Rather you are endowed with the power to create and uncreate, to sense, to know, to understand, and to unify. You can use your faculties to express truth or to express false. There is no limit to what you can create in truth.

We know the error in our logic simply because of what we experience in a false mood. We simply come to the logical conclusions.

For example, we might say to ourselves, "This does not feel good", "This does not feel right", "This makes me feel alone". Fortunately, there is a limit to the deception we can express. There is always a psychological rock bottom; a limit to our ignorance. From there, you can turn your attention to the mood that would be your salvation. But what you are really doing is orienting your mind in the direction of the one-mind: the origin of truth. Truth sets your mind free from the shackles of self-deception.

Every single desirable mood in this book helps you do one thing: the act of moving your attention from false impressions to the source of truth and being aware of the fact that you are part and parcel with it. You are truth aware of your own existence.

As you read this book, notice where your attention moves. Where your attention moves is where your power of being moves. What you decide to focus on becomes the central pattern in your experience. Everything else blurs outs and disappears. So, focus your attention intently on the good, the beautiful, the perfect, and the serene. If the world around you seems to be crumbling, be the source of constructive thought to create a new order. Let the false ideas and concepts that you once assumed true fall away and experience the attainment of excellence.

The attainment of excellence is not some experience in some distant, unknown, and uncertain future held in the hands of another or in a puzzling, invisible power. The attainment of excellence is experiencing oneness with the mood of excellence with your attention. This is a very simple operation.

Every person has this capacity and shares the same power. There is nothing different between you and another person. The only difference is *what* you create in your imagination and give entry into your power of being by your focused attention. The mood you create in your imagination determines what *you* think, feel, and do in *your* own world and when *your* experience converges with others.

Everyone is a distinct self-aware part of the one-mind. We are all connected to each other through the power each and every person *is*. *Everyone* is self-aware, creative and intelligent power. We all shine from the same source.

IDENTIFYING FALSE SELF-CONCEPTIONS

A ll false moods are rooted in a false self-concept.

How you perceive yourself is critical to creative expression and fulfillment.

What you *can* do is a function of what you *accept* as true about your very *nature*.

If you say, for example, that you cannot paint or draw and therefore will not even try to paint or draw, what you are really saying is that you do not have a creative nature and are therefore incapable of expressing it.

When I help people with money, I help them to understand that *managing* money *is* in their nature.

For example, a dear friend never thought she could manage her own wealth. She had lived on the edge of poverty for many years. She had her own business, but earned enough money just to survive. She allowed me to help her grow her awareness in financial management.

I explained to her a very simple observation. I said, "You have been living off your wits and imagination for so long and you have managed very well to survive. The only difference between what you've been making before and what you can make now is *what* you focus your wits and imagination *on*."

I explained to my friend that there is literally no difference between imagining yourself on the verge of poverty and superfluent wealth. It takes the same level of personal power, same use of attention, and same use of imaginal activity to achieve two totally different results. The only difference is the seed by which she based her mood and that was her own self-conception.

After I had helped her find a nice private apartment that met her needs she confessed, "I had never imagined that I could do this."

I asked her, "*Do* what?"

"Live on my own in my own place, pay my own bills, and have a steady job," she replied.

She didn't believe she could *manage* her own finances because she didn't accept that this *capacity* existed entirely within her as a natural way of being.

When doing something is natural to you, it's instinctive and easy. When doing something feels resistant and difficult, it's an opportunity to recognize what false self-concept exists within the arrangement of your mind (e.g. your subconscious mind) that you have accepted as true.

Most work with any coach or therapist or mentor centers around recognizing and releasing false self-concepts that would have you act as if doing things that you want to do are unnatural to you.

Your task during the course of reading this book is recognizing all the false self-concepts that you have accepted as true about yourself that are limiting your ability to *do* what you want. More importantly, the task is to forget those self-concepts entirely.

You can only *do* what you *accept* is true about your own *nature*.

By the end of the book, you will disidentify with many false self-conceptions. You will release all conceptions of limited capacity and function. You will release all deceptive obstructive thinking that would tell you that you can't do anything about the things in your world that are important to you. Even if it is to simply change how you perceive and experience the conditions in your life, you will have gained immensely.

You are a life giving force. You are formless, shapeless awareness. You are connected to the one-mind and thus to all. You share the same capacity of the one-mind to create experiences using your imagination. Experiences always begin as moods because moods are constructed by inner feeling faculties.

By simply directing your attention and commanding your power of being to enter into oneness with an imaginal design based upon your own self-conception you *can* create your own experience. You *can* change how *you* think, how *you* feel, and what *you* do.

Your understanding of the definition of being a life giving force is critical to successful mood engineering because this power of being goes beyond physical limitations, what you can see, and fleeting life conditions.

This self-understanding shifts your entire paradigm of how you go about living because you will have understood your true nature. Your true nature inherently provides you with capacities, capabilities, and understanding that supersede all false thoughts and false self-concepts.

In short: you are capable of much more and endowed with much more than you can presently conceive from your current self-concept.

You must accept the truth of this immutable fact and assume your true nature if you are to accomplish all that you are capable of doing.

Perform this activity to identify and release false self-concepts:

Step 1: Observe the feelings in your body-mind. These are the sensations of your present mood.

Example:

Step 1:	
Tight	
Compressed	
Can't breath	
Squeezed	
Out of breath	
Rigid	
Stuck	
Holding on	
Contracted	

Step 2: Write down the *opposite* feeling of the present mood. You cannot get this wrong. Write what immediately comes to mind.

Example:

Step 1:	**Step 2:**
Tight	*Flexible*
Compressed	*Expressed*
Can't breath	*Breathe*
Squeezed	*Open;released*
Out of breath	*Oxygenated*
Rigid	*Movement*
Stuck	*Active*
Holding on	*Receiving*
Contracted	*Expanded*

Step 3: Write down *what* these feelings are telling you that you are presently aware of being. This is your mood.

Step 1:	Step 2:
Tight	*Flexible*
Compressed	*Expressed*
Can't breath	*Breathe*
Squeezed	*Open; Released*
Out of breath	*Oxygenated*
Rigid	*Movement*
Stuck	*Active*
Holding on	*Receiving*
Contracted	*Expanded*
Step 3:	
Because, these feelings tell me that I am presently aware of being <u>*Overwhelmed*</u>	

Step 4: This mood you currently find yourself aware of being is telling you your present self-conception. Write down what this mood is indicating that you presently accept is true about your own nature.

Step 1:	Step 2:
Tight	*Flexible*
Compressed	*Expressed*
Can't breath	*Breathe*
Squeezed	*Open; Released*
Out of breath	*Oxygenated*
Rigid	*Movement*
Stuck	*Active*
Holding on	*Receiving*
Contracted	*Expanded*
Step 3:	
Because, these feelings tell me that I am presently aware of being *Overwhelmed*	
Step 4:	
Because, I am: <u>**Limited**</u>	

Step 5: Look at step 3 and 4 and write down the exact opposite of the mood and self-concept. This is the truth of your nature.

You will see the false feelings, mood, and self-concept in the left column and the true feelings, mood, and self-concept in the right column.

Step 1:	Step 2:
Tight	*Flexible*
Compressed	*Expressed*
Can't breath	*Breathe*
Squeezed	*Open; Released*
Out of breath	*Oxygenated*
Rigid	*Movement*
Stuck	*Active*
Holding on	*Receiving*
Contracted	*Expanded*
Step 3:	**Step 5:**
Because, these feelings tell me that I am presently aware of being <u>Overwhelmed</u>	**I am now aware of feeling <u>magnanimous.</u>**
Step 4:	
Because, I am: <u>Limited</u>	**Because I am: <u>Unstoppable.</u>**

As you can see from this exercise, the logic goes that if you are formless, shapeless awareness that is a life-giving force then you are in fact unstoppable.

Therefore, you would take on the form of magnanimity (the etymology of the word is *great soul*) and you would emanate feelings of flexibility, movement, and activeness as listed in the right column.

This simple process of logical examination can be done in moments. I have outlined this step-by-step process for you so that you can practice it. Apply this process every time you find yourself feeling an undesired mood. You will eventually be so good at moving attention from mood to mood that you will notice how long you can sustain a desirable mood.

With time, you will notice how little you find yourself in an undesirable mood because your self-concept will remain constantly oriented towards the one-mind and aligned with your true nature.

Remember feelings do not tell you who you are. They only tell you what you are thinking. What you are thinking tells you where your attention is oriented. Change your orientation and change your experience.

QUALITIES OF MIND THAT FORM THE QUALITY OF YOUR WORLD

The quality of the assumptions upon which you build your inner world of experience becomes your outer world of experience.

Every thought form impressed upon your power of being becomes animated and experienced *first* by you and then projected into your outer world of experience.

That is why it is impossible to think a hateful, critical, condescending thought without *first* experiencing the quality of such thoughts. Every pattern of experience must first be expressed *in* and ultimately *through* you.

The instrument you call your physical body is the pattern multiplier and the formation of the thoughts you permit to enter into the temple which is your inner experience is reflected in your DNA, cellular structure, your neural network, your organ tissue structure and ultimately becomes seen in the outer world of experience.

I changed my entire life experience when I fully understood this concept. I made a vow to myself that I would never again allow myself to accept and therefore dwell upon false thought forms which are all emanations of self-centered thoughts of separation and division.

As long as I saw myself as separate from everyone, I produced thoughts of loneliniess, hatred, discrimination, fear, anxiety, and confusion. I experienced these thoughts through my feeling capacities, saw these thoughts in my imagination, and worried as long as I dwelled upon and accepted these thoughts as truth of my nature.

If you want to change your life experience from the inside out, you must master your mood. You must assume the qualities of your true nature. You are formless, shapeless awareness that is the living expression of creative intelligence - eternal, powerful, unlimited, and entirely capable. When you leave the instrument you call your physical body it is your presence that departs. Thus, how is it possible to identify with an instrument when you are the animating intelligence that is part and parcel of all animating intelligence?

The moment that you identify with an object that you see with your physical eyes, or identify with a thought you've heard, or identify with a clump of cells, you have confined yourself to that which you accept as true of your nature. Undesirable moods simply work to show you what you accept is true about your natural state of being and the quality of thoughts from the role you have decided to play.

You can tell what is true and false simply by the fruits of the moods you experience. It is true that all people are honest. They cannot deceive themselves longer than the point they have reached the logical end of a false thought. The moment you realize that you got it wrong, you can't go back. And, frankly, nothing feels as good as knowing you were wrong because that's when you start to think and feel in alignment with the truth of your true nature.

When I say that all people are honest it is that they cannot help but express that which they are aware of being - that which they assume is their true nature. It is in this compulsion of honesty that we express the moods in which we dwell.

Sooner or later, the fruit of your moods will ripen and they will harden into your outer worldly experience. Before you know it, you and the entire world will know that which you have dwelt upon in secret. You will be rewarded with the fruits of your moods in the open.

There is a fundamental difference between honesty and truthfulness. Honesty is the only mode of expression we all have and it displays your moods in the fullness of expression in your physical body, mental environment, spoken words, and actions.

Truthfulness is based upon objective, non-negotiable, non-rationalizable truth of ultimate reality: We are all one. All is one.

You are part and parcel of the all encompassing power of creative, intelligent life.

There is no one in the world who can disprove this fact for even in attempting to disprove this fact one must use the faculties of mind that we *all* share: imagining, thinking, feeling, decision making and the power of being in order to experience any process of thought. We cannot escape this fact of reality.

We are coming into greater understanding of this truth so that we may dispel all illusions of separation and division. There are small minded people who attempt to gain the entire world and lose conscious touch with their soul by creating and perpetuating illusions and organizations based upon this deception of mind. Even then, when these people meet the end of their experience in this world, they too go back and enter into fullness of oneness once again.

This is why it is important to release all identification with objects, organizations, temporary and passing conditions, race beliefs, class systems, gender roles, religions, institutions and all such constructions in the outer world of experience.

No, this does not mean to sell your belongings and move to a commune or ashram in some isolated location. It means to release the hold they have over your attention, your power of being, and your choices. It means to release the hold they have over your innate ability to turn your attention to and dwell in your power of being. For, when you do you will experience oneness. You will experience oneness with the qualities of being that are expressed in one-mind. Desirable moods are simply qualities of the one-mind, in the fullness of oneness. When you enter into oneness with your attention you will never again allow yourself to be separated from the perfection of this experience. And, it never has to end.

People chase emotional highs through drugs, alcohol, sex, accolades, possession, and power. As soon as we experience the event that we believe would give us the mood we desire to experience, it slips right out of our hands. We can construct anything in our imagination and experience it in its ephemerality in the outer world. An event does not tell you who you are. So, to wait for such an experience to affirm to you that you are smart, successful, beautiful, or loveable is to wait in vain.

It takes a higher understanding to acknowledge that moods do not result from external experiences, but rather internal arrangements of mind. Thus, to experience continual positivity one must be the embodiment of positivity by nature; not condition our mood upon the manifestation of an event that promises to make us feel positive.

When you master your mood, no condition can determine for you what you feel. For, you understand and embody your true nature. Nothing you see with your eyes, hear with your ears, or observe with your sensing faculties can turn your attention from your true sense of being.

It is *you* that experiences everything you accept as true about your nature. You must first feel in experience the emotions of condemnation. You must first feel in experience the emotions of anguish. You must first feel in experience the emotions of greed. What you give to the world - every word that comes out of your mouth, every hormonal secretion you produce with your physical body, every subconscious behavioral impulse - must first be experienced by you.

So, if you are to create better experiences and therefore build a better world, you must attune your attention wholly upon the truth of your nature and be animated by it. For, in doing so, you save yourself from the limitations and confinement of all false thoughts and temporary conditions. You will never again be led astray by a false prophet promising you salvation when you can very well do so yourself by simply moving your attention to your true nature: oneness.

Moods

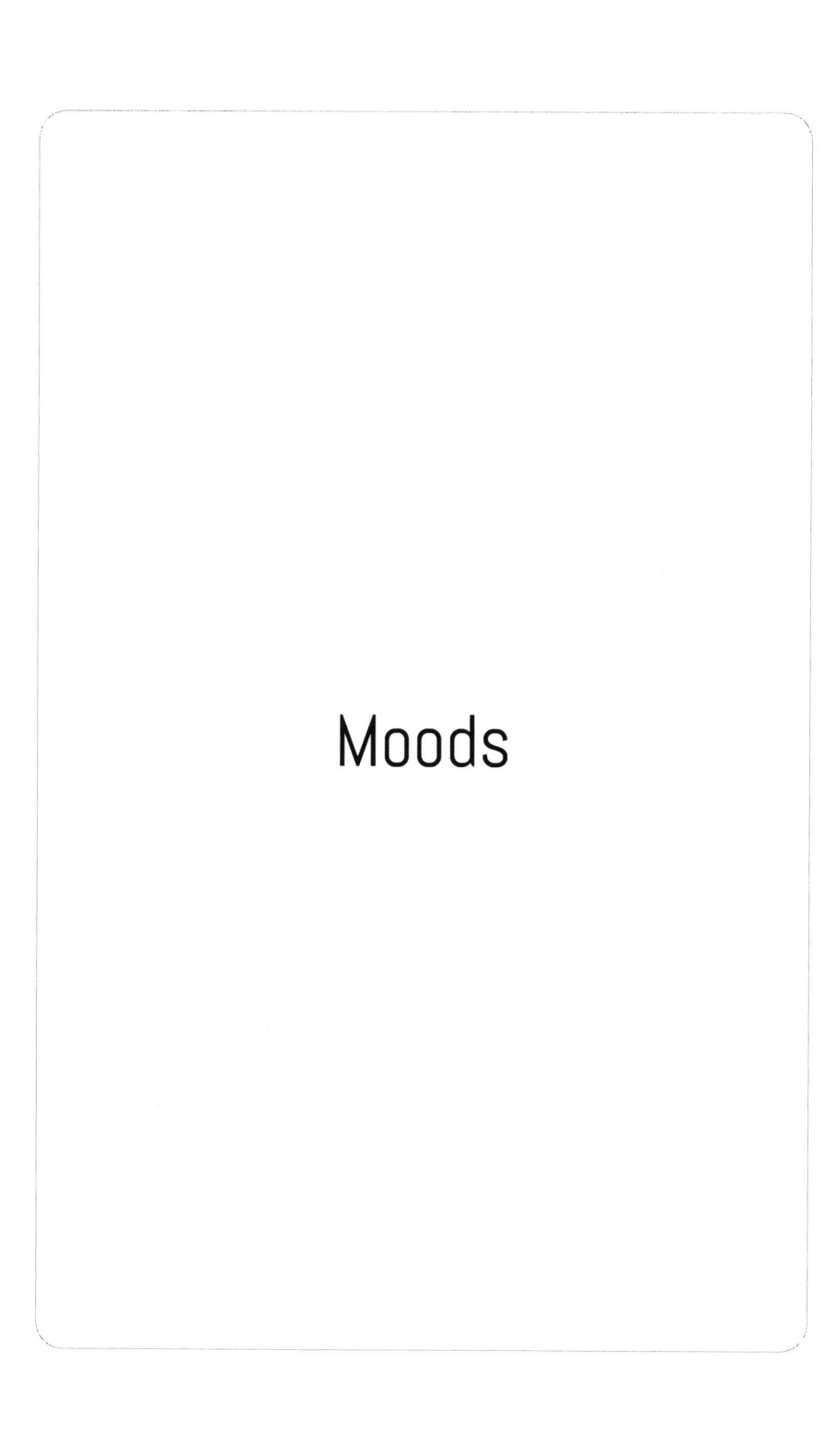

A
Abduction - Absolution

I give myself absolution.

I absolve myself of all false and deceptive thinking.

The power of my being absolves all misunderstanding and illusions.

Absolution is boundaryless freedom.

Absolution is the freedom to roam without threat of paralysis and confinement.

There is no external decision maker who determines where I go or what I do.

My past is behind me and I alone decide what I accomplish.

I feel certainty and I am directed with the knowledge that no barriers exist between me and my destination.

The instrument I call my physical body is my own. My experiences are my own.

Absolution emanates relief in my body.

Every part of me is at ease and I feel the power of my being circulating.

The instrument I call my physical body is warm and self-contained.

I feel my ease of being in the knowing that I was, am, and will always be free.

Ache - Soothe

The power of my being is smooth and calm.

Soothing, gentle, calming energy spreads throughout the instrument I call my physical body.

My mind feels calm and unburdened.

Soothing energy fulfills the completion of all tasks.

I hear good news and pleasant tidings.

Harmonious music and natural sounds fill my environment.

Everyone gets along and works together with ease, soothing collected minds.

The power of my being is quiet and productive in a manner in which results are guaranteed.

The power of my being is the easy achievement of goals in a timely manner.

Protection and direction shelter my steps.

My attention floats down a gentle stream of thought.

Affected - Cleansed

Everlasting purity flows out of the one-mind. I cleanse and renew the arrangement of my mind of all false impressions accepted by behavior I witness. I only allow loving actions to impress upon my mind. I am renewed by the purity of my being. I do not identify with feelings I experience. I do not identify with thoughts.

I disengage my feeling capacities from all false impressions. I relieve myself of all internalized burdens. I wash myself clean of all false feelings. I cleanse my mind of all deceptive thinking and false premises.

I cleanse my memory of all false impressions. I have always been as I am now: free, clean, and whole.

I recognize the purity and innocence of my being. I absolve myself of all harmful thinking that caused harmful behavior. I immediately turn to my imagination to create new, beautiful thoughts that restore visions of integrity and wholeness in my experience.

I turn my attention to the origin of grace, mercy, and forgiveness. I extend to all parties grace, mercy, and forgiveness for that which I extend to others must be first felt and experienced by me.

I accept the truth that the power in me has the ability to cleanse the arrangement of my mind and perfect all of my experiences. I accept the truth that the power of my being has the ability to guide my attention in a perfect way and to experience life perfectly.

I am done with past habits of thinking. I am done with past habits. I free myself from all mental limitations. I am done with remembering errors in logic. I look forward into my future and see visions of wholeness, integrity, and expansive glory.

Aggravate - Alleviate

The power of my being removes heavy burdens. The arrangement of my mind is clear and centered.

My body is used in the correct manner for the correct purposes.

I feel good in my body with perfect poise.

Alleviating pulsations in my body deliver oxygenated blood to aching muscles.

The power of my being releases laughter and sighs of relief upon the receipt of good news that I construct in my imagination.

I expect positive events to occur.

I see myself with understanding through all eyes.

The awareness of truth alleviates all misunderstanding.

I always find what I seek.

I give the power of my being permission to accomplish all that is my good.

Events follow the direction of attention and occur in my favor.

Aggravated - Relieved

I feel joyful thoughts. I employ my mental faculties for the fulfillment of delightful purposes.

I perform activities that are pleasing to me when I want to do them. I am supported in my autonomy and individuality. I use my days according to the purpose that I have defined for them. Essential tasks are finished and my world is complete.

Everything and everyone around me is self-sustaining and regulating.

Situations meet their joyful end which opens up new, happy opportunities.

Happiness is available to me now instead of in the future. Resources are available and accessible now and are at my complete disposal.

All doors are open for me to choose and knowing which one to choose because that door has been designed for me by the Origin of all Being.

I rest well and wake up feeling refreshed and invigorated.

My body moves in perfect harmony with my mind, healthy and strong.

Aggression - Gentle

The gentleness of oneness supports me.

I feel softness and smoothness in the temple of my inner world. I sense warmth and caring.

I feel the gentle presence of my being.

I progress steadily in a forward momentum.

I move easily and experience a progressive stream of perfect thought.

I merge my attention into oneness with all that is my good.

I am united and understand everything in my awareness with full competency.

I am articulate, intelligent awareness that effectively pierces all illusion.

I am gracious and graceful.

I am calm and effective. I recognize the existence of self-evident truth.

I feel the warmth of my own presence.

I release from the total arrangement of my mind impure thoughts and deceptive in manners of thinking.

Agitated - Enjoy

The joy of my being expresses itself through thought and action.

I see with my mind's eye beautiful images that evoke appreciation, elation, jubilation, and relief.

The peaceful power of my being dissolves all false growths and constructions from my world.

The joy of my being disarms all. The joy of my being relaxes all.

The joy of my being reorients all in my presence towards the origin of all joy.

I feel the oneness in all. I feel the perfection in all. I recognize the innocence, unconditioned and perfect power that dwells in all.

I laugh with ease. I move and dance with pleasure.

I feel the perfection of oneness.

I recognize the harmony inherent in me and amplify that with the instrument I call my physical body.

I delight in the intelligence and creativity in me. I regard all experiences as the perfect fulfillment of my good.

The power of my being contains and emanates endless appreciation, adoration, and recognition of oneness.

I feel the goodness of my nature. I feel the goodness inherent in all perfect forms.

Alone - Together

I strip away all isolating, alienating thoughts from the total arrangement of my mind that would have me falsely accept the idea that I am not part and parcel of the one-mind and thus connected to all.

I feel into the depths of my being to reach for and touch the sensations of comfort, camaraderie, togetherness, and friendship.

I can feel the pulsation of oneness in all and I recognize the natural propensity to share in the feeling of joy that being together in distinction and oneness brings.

I appreciate the distinction expressed through every self-aware part of the one-mind and remain fully cognizant of our shared heritage of being.

I see through all illusions of division.

I see past all attempts to dissuade me of my oneness with all. I ignore the spektre of false threats.

All are one. All are together. We are united, unified, connected, and everlastingly one.

Anger - Stillness

I sense the stillness of my being. I sense the firm centeredness of my being that forms stability in my experience.

I observe with clarity and neutrality. I sense accurately and touch gently. I understand fully all that enters into my awareness.

With steady flowing movement I touch with grace, calm, and openness.

I feel the power of my being circulating and flowing through the instrument I call my physical body. I feel the pulsation of the one-mind synchronizing the beat of my heart. I breathe fully. The instrument I call my physical body is oxygenated with revitalizing currents of intelligent thought.

I rest in the stillness of the one-mind. I put down all burdens and turn my attention to the bounty, expanse, and splendor of my inherent majesty.

I release all conditioned thinking. I release all false thoughtforms from the arrangement of my mind. All illusions fall away from my mind's eye.

In my imagination, I revise memories deemed unacceptable to me. I create new visions of fulfillment, success, and accomplishment. I recreate my mental landscape to scenes of serenity, magnanimity, vibrance, and perfection.

I sense the perfect construction of my mind connected to the one-mind. I receive wisdom, clarity, and instruction for the fulfillment of my good in my world.

I sense the perfecting, organizing presence of the one-mind correcting all false thoughts. My physical body amplifies patterns of relief, ease, and rest. I witness feelings of pleasure and jubilance moving through my body and into my world. All is well.

Anguish - Certainty

With the power of my being I create my experiences. With the power of my being I can feel the good inherent to my nature.

In self-understanding I recognize my capacity to create imaginal designs that would become my experience in my outer world.

In my inner world I can feel the reality and completion of all imaginal designs for they are accomplished in one-mind and perfect in their design and ready for immediate expression through me.

I hold within my imagination the recognition and fulfillment of perfect forms of inner experience.

I direct my attention and master my creative facilities to the immediate fulfillment of perfect experiences.

The power of my being is certain, correct, perfect, unstoppable and immediately moves all patterns of form for the fulfillment of my good.

I expect perfect fulfillment for the one-mind never fails. The vastness, eternality, and intelligence of the one-mind performs all accomplished states in perfect succession.

Each moment is perfectly made to show me the quality and pattern of my thoughts. Because there is no other function by which all experiences are formed, I am certain of the results as I am sure of the thoughts that I feel within the depths of my inner experience.

I feel certain because I am singular. I am one. And I impregnate my inner world with that which I affix my attention. In singularity and in unwavering connection, I enter into oneness with those thoughts that are acceptable to me. As I do so, I enter into greater awareness of the vastness of experience that is inherent in one-mind.

Annoying - Fluid

I can sense the fluidity and flexibility of my power of being.

I am suspended in the malleable power of oneness. I feel supported, directed, accompanied by creative intelligent power at all times that goes before me and makes ways that are unseen in the outer world of experience.

I steady my attention upon the firm pathway created for me on which I easily progress.

I feel the fulfillment of my nature expressing itself through my mental faculties and the instrument I call my physical body.

I am at peace with all. I am at peace within the core of my being.

I reorient my attention to the place designated for me in one-mind. I direct my mind to experience and express stillness, serenity, wisdom, and creative intelligence.

The power of my being is not limited by outer conditions. The power of my being is not limited by the actions of others that are based upon false premises that reject the truth of our true nature.

I sense the coordinating intelligent power of my being circulating throughout all. I observe this power and engage with it so that my decisions are in alignment with perfect understanding.

I release all habits of mind that seek to control the actions of others. I release all deceptive thinking that would have me accept the mood of powerlessness. I access the power of my being to clear away all false thoughtforms rooted in the rejection of truth.

Anxiety - Calm

I judiciously choose the direction I send my attention. I, with full power and authority over my own mental faculties, feel after sensations and patterns of serenity, stillness, and steadfastness.

There is no other source of power over the faculties of my mind and the instrument I call my physical body.

I banish all false thoughts from the presence of my mind.

I destroy all delusions by turning my attention and revoking my consent from all false thoughts and false forms.

All false conditions immediately dissolve at my command. With confidence, I direct my inner experience to conform to the perfect pattern of the one-mind.

I withdraw all the power of my being I have given to construct false thoughtforms. I withdraw all the power of my being from all activity that perpetuates false constructions.

I am stabled. I am centered. I am deeply rooted in the fortifying fortress of oneness.

All my affairs are settled. My mind is settled. All is well in me.

I feel the stillness of my being. I feel the stillness of oneness. I see the clarity of my world.

Apart - United

I am united with my imaginal designs. I think of the object or presence I want to bring into my experience and dwell on it until the characteristics of the object or presence come clearly to mind. I can feel the object or presence inside of myself. I can viscerally feel the presence of that which I intend to bring into experience.

I am one with the force that brings all into experience. The intelligence of the one-mind seals the instructions into all parties required to bring about the expression of my inner sensations. What I sense with my imagination always comes into expression in the outer world of form. I am united with my good always, now, and forever.

The instrument I call my physical body is propelled by the creative forces that bring movement to the entire universe. I am part of the mind that directs the movements of the entire universe. Thus, I am capable of using my attention to create my world by harnessing the creative elements of the one-mind.

I cannot fail in realizing my inner sensations. I only create those experiences that are acceptable and pleasing to me. Every day is an expression of one-mind experiencing the imaginal sensations felt in self. I choose inner sensations that feel truthful.

I impress upon the subconscious mind sensations that are reflective of the origin of truth so that I may know myself as I am. When I say I am, I feel my truest, original sense of self. I feel the pure, intelligent power of my true self that animates the creative elements with instructions for self-fulfillment.

Argue - Resolve

There is no conflict in one-mind. All that is real is true.

I know what to accept as true.

I feel truth with my sensing faculties. I recognize truth and all its qualities.

I am at peace within my being.

I feel resolved to orient my attention to truth in all its forms.

Answers to all my questions are readily available to me.

The truth is self-evident in all experiences. I can recognize the truth no matter the condition, illusion, or false construction.

I am certain of all that is good. I feel certainty within the depths of my being.

I see past all illusions, deceptions, false statements of fact, and fleeting conditions.

I will not be deceived. I will not be distracted.

All disputes dissolve in my presence. All conflicts fade in the light of truth.

I bring clarity, peace, serenity into all experiences with ideas containing solutions.

I reach for higher truths. I feel for perfect constructions of thought.

Every answer is available to me. Every solution is apparent to me. I understand with ease and simplicity.

Arrogant - Equal

I recognize the perfect presence of the one-mind in all.

There is no battle, there is no fight, there is no scourge in oneness. There is only perfection in one-mind.

I feel my ceaseless, boundaryless, infinite connection with all. All are one.

All share the same faculties of mind. All are capable of great works with the power of their being. I can see more than temporary conditions. I understand the workings of the one-mind in action.

I feel peace in my inner world of being. Express peace in every interaction and in every experience.

The power of my being dissolves all illusions of separation, division, and otherness.

I feel the equality of endowment in all.

I am aware of the assumptions that form the arrangement of my mind. I am not my mind. I am my true nature and that is to express the quality of oneness in my experience.

I see all distinct self-aware parts of the one-mind for who they really are. I release and abandon all assumptions of imperfection, decay, morbidity, and disease.

I turn my attention away from deceptive thoughts and orient my attention to the eternal truth of my being.

Attack - Bless

Each and every single thought that enters into the temple of my inner world affirms truth.

I only experience thoughts rooted in the bliss and clarity of truth. I only conceive of imaginal designs that are patterned after perfection.

I feel perfect oneness in my experience and direct that pattern through the chamber of my inner world and into my outer world of experience.

I access thoughts that evoke feelings of serenity, appreciation, togetherness, and recognition of the indwelling power and presence inherent in all.

I speak words that affirm progress. I speak words that affirm understanding and unity. I visualize acts that recognize and preserve the integrity inherent to all.

I see past all illusions created by false assumptions. I deny authority in false powers. I choose to experience the grandeur of oneness and to speak words that orient all attention to this quality of being.

I use my words to command the appearance of all that is acceptable to me in my experience. I dispel all false authority.

I sense the authority of the one-mind inherent in me. No false thought, concept, or construction can continue to exist in the light of truth.

Avoid - Attend

I am always surrounded in my experience by the everlasting power of the one-mind that is the core of my being. I feel the intelligent, loving presence of oneness emanating in my inner world throughout my outer world.

I am present. I stand firmly in my presence. I stand resolutely confident in the power of my being.

I remain unaffected from all false impressions. I remain resolutely aware of the power of my being at all times.

In complete liberty of being, I resign myself to stay aware of my connection to all. I can attend any experience and render it whole and perfect. I can enter into any experience and perfect it by the loving presence of my being.

I remain illumined by the power of my being. I retain my joy through all circumstances of thought and experience.

There is no external power. There is no external mind. There is only one power and one mind. That power and mind lives and dwells in me for I am part and parcel with the whole and origin of all.

Nothing can frighten me. Nothing can control the direction of my attention. I am singularly focused upon visions of truth. I am motivated by pure designs. I act on and habituate feelings of purity.

The pattern in me is perfect and whole. I recognize its completeness and harmony with all. I am creative, intelligent, and self-aware power. I exercise the power of my being to create and fulfill goodness in my experience. All is well.

B
Bad - Understood

Understanding permeates the entire universe. Understanding exists within me. That is why I can intuitively understand anything and anyone. Understanding is at the center of my awareness. I see with understanding. I feel with understanding. I know with understanding.

Understanding is my ability to recognize the truth inherent in all. Understanding is an inherent aspect of my everlasting connection with the origin of all thought. Inside of every thought is the pattern for its expression. I instantly understand all that enters into my awareness. I can express understanding with simple observation. I can hear truth emanating from all conditions. I can see with understanding patterns of thought and their logical conclusions.

I cannot be deceived. I cannot be subject to delusion. I know the truth because I recognize the truth. I fulfill the truth in everything I do. I recognize the truth of all parties.

Who I am is centered power that amplifies and magnifies all thoughts. My being is absolute. My being is eternal and will outlive the coming and going of any thought form. I am greater than any thoughtform. I will outlast any condition. All things pass away in my presence of being. I create and destroy conditions by moving my attention.

I understand who I am. I understand what I am. I will not be defined by false thinking. I will not be deceived by the false thoughts of other self-aware parts of the one-mind. I regain feelings of stability on the foundation of the truth of my being.

I am inherently good. I am inherently loving. I am inherently beautiful and free. Nothing can change this fact, even if false assumptions claim otherwise.

I will not dwell upon false thoughts. I do not allow false thoughts to dwell in my mind.

I give power and form to truth in my experience. I correct all erroneous thinking and habits with higher concepts of truth. I only participate in activities that affirm the truth. I am aware of my sovereignty of mind.

I exercise my sovereignty of mind by thinking of only the truth. I understand at all times. I reflect understanding to all people. I only speak with understanding and act with understanding. I gain understanding at all times.

Barriers - Infinite

I survey the environment around me and wander and roam in any direction I choose.

I, expanding into every direction, am free and clear. My heart is open and expansive. My breath expands the instrument I call my body. I feel bigger and larger than all the tasks that I endeavor.

Each step I take is light, steady, and firm.

The ground beneath me is solid and unfolds around me. In every direction I go. I feel embraced by life, by myself, and all as one.

Nothing can stop me from feeling like my pure self.

Effortlessly, I get bigger and bigger, growing and growing ever more into the infiniteness of space and time. Ideas come endlessly and ceaselessly to me in a joyful, enlightening fashion.

I feel myself grasping good ideas and knowledge that allows me to power forward in my chosen and intended direction.

My joy is infinite because I am infinite joy. I morph into anything I choose and I love the process of evolving.

I have fun being me and sharing me with others who see and feel my presence. Being me comes naturally to me and others enjoy who I am.

Boundless joy spreads into every possible direction of my life, giving me a sense of security and accomplishment. I am grateful for my infinite presence and the harmony I feel with all creation. I am infinite peace and abundance of being.

Behind - On Time

I am on time. My heart beats in perfect unison with the heartbeat of the Origin of all Order. I abide by the law and the law guides me.

I arrive on time. I complete my tasks on time. I make progress on long term goals on time. I experience daily tasks on time.

My mind and body operate in rhythm with the seasons and evolution of my mind. All is accomplished in perfect order and at its appointed hour. I go through life with ease, comfort, and stillness.

I fulfill my duties with joy and ease. I move from one task to another and feel satisfied with my contributions and progress for the day. I give each day my best and know when to stop, rest, pause, and move forward.

I know what to do and know when to do it. My intuition guides me to the fulfillment of my good. My mind and body move in unison with my good. I rest when I need to rest, I act when I need to act, I sleep when I need to sleep.

I move at my own perfect pace and all that is my good is accomplished at that pace. I accomplish my goals and experience my good is the exact age that I am supposed to be. I feel good where I am and everywhere I go. I meet specific people at their appointed hour.

No matter what I do or what choice I make, I know that I accomplish and fulfill my good. Everything I do from start to finish begins and ends on time.

Blame - Mercy

There is no external cause. There is no external power. There is no external mind.

There is only one-mind. There is only oneness.

I take responsibility for my actions. I take responsibility for my choices. I take responsibility for my attitudes. I take responsibility for my moods. I take responsibility for how I experience the events and conditions in my world of experience.

I absolve all for the misuse of mental faculties.

I absolve all for the rejection of their true nature.

I absolve all for acting under the influence of a false mood.

I do not identify with prior actions. I do not identify with false and temporary conditions. I do not identify with systems of thought created by superstitious and deceptive thinking.

I free myself from all limitations. I free myself from all obstructions.

I give myself permission to enter into oneness with the everlasting peace of the one-mind.

I see myself in the fabric of unity with all.

All are in their perfect place of being. All is well in the temple of my inner world.

Block - Pump

The pulse of the one-mind pervades all distinct self-aware parts.

The pulse of the infinite, expansive, boundaryless presence of the one-mind inhabits all worlds.

Noone can stop, prevent, slow down, restrict, or imprison the presence of my being.

No false thoughts of obstruction, limitation, restriction, and boundaries can stop the intelligent creativity in the power of my being from growing, expanding, and coming into the fullness of expression.

No boundaries exist in one-mind. All is one.

No limitations exist in one-mind. All is one.

No threat exists in one-mind. All is one.

No barrier of mind can prevent the expansion of my true nature.

No organization based upon the rejection of truth shall remain. No false growth may inhabit my mind. I dissolve all false words, thoughts, feelings, and attitudes of mind.

I feel the intelligent, restorative power of my being coursing through the instrument I call my physical body. I feel the pulsation of vitality emanating throughout my physical body.

My body-mind is in perfect harmony with the one-mind. I am at peace, resting in the presence of oneness.

Bothered - Resolute

I resolutely use my power for good. There is no other use or purpose for which the power of my being may be appropriated. Every assumption in my mind is based upon truth, the awareness of truth, and the application of truth in my experience.

I give to my imagination every possible beautiful, kind, and expansive thought to feed on. My imagination grows from the planting of truth in my consciousness.

I dispel every false word. I dissolve every false image and assumption about myself, other parties, and the one-mind. False thoughts dissolve from my being. All false conceptions and constructions (feelings, thoughtforms, deceptions) are immediately emptied of all power and organization.

I feed upon good thoughts. I dwell upon true thoughts. I turn my attention away from false thoughts. I am strengthened and resolved with power that is calm, organized, and steady.

Every part of my experience is serene. Every part of my future is certainly good. Every part of my memories are seen with loving understanding.

I do not fear. I do not dread any false image and false mood. I declare with the might of my power resolution, solutions, and peace.

Every experience I have is good. Every opportunity for me is good. I know when to ignore and disregard a false condition. I know when to transform it with my imagination. I do not give power of acceptance in any false thoughtform or conception. I resign myself to sit on the throne of truth. From which, with the highest perspective, I create the kingdom of my world.

Bound - Spread

There is no limit to the power of my being.

There is no capacity of mind that I cannot express.

The power of my being, my eternal sense of oneness, connects intelligently and masterfully to all and is capable of all tasks I send for it to accomplish.

My attention can go anywhere I send it. My attention can touch all manner of form and can enter into any structure of mind.

The power of my being traverses all distances.

I can see any place in my mind's eye.

I can touch any distinct self-aware part of the one-mind with the connection I feel and share with all parties.

I feel like my true self at all times.

All doors are open for me. All paths are laid for me. All places are open to me.

Burdened - Belong

I am fundamental to my experience.

Without my intelligent presence nothing can be experienced.

I am essential. I am vital. I am at the center of my experiences. Without me all experiences are impossible.

Thus, I belong to the one-mind for the individuation, completion, and fullest expression of the perfection that is the one-mind.

Without my participation no form may be given expression. Thus, I withdraw my participation from all deceptive conditions and interactions based on falsities.

I only employ the power of my being for the fulfillment of truth.

I disengage my attention from all captive thoughtforms and all unions based upon lies.

I am the embodiment of ease. I am the embodiment of creative power. I transform all false images, memories, and conceptions with the activation of my imagination and direction of my thoughts. I engage my imagination in constructing beautiful creations, inventive solutions, and open passageways that expand my knowledge of oneness.

All is well in me. All is good in me. The richness of creation is in the power of my being and with the power of my being I set my attention free to experience all that expresses liberation, expansion, and growth.

Burn - Glide

I am weightless light. I am pure, unadulterated power. I feel the power of my presence and its lifting, organizing intelligence.

Every part of the instrument I call my physical body works in harmony with each other. My entire mind is in unison and in alignment with the one-mind. I feel the pulsation of the one-mind in my heart. This pulsation continues throughout my entire body, filling my physical body with rejuvenating, reinvigorating patterns. The pulsation of this power renews every cell, neuron, and gland. I feel healthy. I feel good.

I sense my body-mind renewing itself at all times. I always feel at ease, gliding through every experience in my world. I am weightless, self-aware, creative, and intelligent power. I am one with the one-mind and the origin of all health.

I sense the vitality of my physical body because I am aware of the vitality that ever renews the arrangement of my mind. I feel the circulation of love throughout my body. It cures all false conditions.

Love is the sensation of oneness living and dwelling in us.

I apply the truth to every false condition. There is no other power that operates my mind. Thus, there is no other power that operates the instrument I call my body.

I feel good all the time because I sense after good all the time. I sense after good all the time because my mind is directly connected to the one-mind.

I am aware of my connection with the one-mind and the indwelling intelligent power in me that operates the functions of my mind and mind-body.

My mind operates perfectly. My physical body reflects this perfect operation.

C
Clench - Open

The bounty and goodness of oneness is available to me.

Every place in mind is open to me.

I release all illusions of blockages and barriers.

All tension dissolves at my command. I feel the warmth and comfort of my being circulating and rejuvenating the instrument I call my physical body.

I let go of all fear. I let go of all false assumptions.

I feel the pulsation of warmth pumping through the instrument I call my physical body.

My heart amplifies the pattern of perfect oneness. I feel the appreciation of all radiating throughout my world.

I express the joy of being.

I orient my attention to oneness and feel the bliss of being within me.

I let go of all patterns of pain. I let go of all burdensome thoughts. I open my mind to receive all that is my good.

My physical body radiates harmony. My physical body is quiet. My body-mind is collected, organized, and connected to the origin of intelligent creativity.

I am open to new ideas. I am open to new ways of thinking. I am open to all that is my good.

I open my attention to recognize that all is within the power of my being.

Complain - Notice

I am capable of noticing the events and conditions around me without allowing myself to be conditioned nor affected by what I observe.

I am able to notice my internal experiences without giving them dominion over my actions.

I am able to notice the behaviors and attitudes of others without concern.

I am able to notice events in stillness, calm, and serenity. I am able to experience my true nature in fullness of expression.

I release all conditioned thought processes. I release all conditioned behavior.

I live and dwell in the ecstasy of my true nature. I am mentally free and expansive.

I release all holds of my attention and dwell upon the harmony and vitality of my being.

I see the light of my being and feel the radiating power that transforms all false conditions into simplicity.

I notice the beauty, simplicity, and organization of life. I notice life unfolding at a gentle pace. I take my time to notice, savor, and fully experience all the grandeur, excellence, and perfection of experience. Each experience is perfect, bright, and colorful. My mind is clear of obstructive thinking, limitations of sensation, and false thoughtforms. I sense and experience my true nature in perfection.

Compression - Extension

I am expansive. I am intelligent power that has given itself form.

I am creative intelligence capable of moving my attention to any plane of thought and to any dimension of relative proximity.

I expand and extend my awareness beyond the dimensions of my physical body-mind. I enlarge my presence and enter into any experience as a distinct self-aware mind.

I enter into any point in space and immediately become aware of the distinct pattern that forms the energy in that space.

I feel myself going beyond the limitations of my present understanding and stretching into higher concepts of truth.

I am unlimited. I am boundless. I am boundaryless.

I extend my attention to any place - I cannot be confined, I cannot be contorted to fit into any pattern of mind that I do not find acceptable to me.

I cannot be contained by limited thinking and false thoughts.

I will not deviate my mind from the origin of truth for I rest in everlasting connection with the power of my being.

I will not use my power to create false thoughtforms.

I dissolve all false thoughtforms in my entire body-mind.

I cleanse myself of conditioned thinking, renewing and restoring my body-mind to higher functions.

Condemn - Appreciate

Appreciation is the magnification of the good inherent in all and in me.

I notice the good inherent in myself and in others.

Appreciation is the magnification of the one-mind that lives and dwells in all parties.

I magnify the presence of good in my mind. Because of this movement of attention, good is enhanced and increased in my experience.

I am free from doubtful thinking that limits the expression of good in my experience. All that I have is good because all that I am is good.

I magnify feelings of joy in my experience. I magnify feelings of stability in my experience. I magnify feelings of excellence in my experience.

Goodness grows in my experience because I am granted and endowed with goodness in all manners of experience.

Thoughts of happiness obliterate false thought forms.

Conditioned - Unconditioned

I am unconditioned consciousness.

I am free from undesirable impressions and limitations that enter into my mind. They are merely formations of mental patterns, they do not tell me who I am; only what I am thinking.

I let go of false mental patterns. I deny ephemeral conditions. I let all thoughts come and go like waves washing in and out of a beach.

I focus my mind on the pure landscape that is my mind. I impress upon my mind only that which is beautiful, harmonious, and serene. I impress upon my mind all concepts rooted in the everlasting wells of truth. In this state, every part of my body-mind is rejuvenated, reinvigorated, and constantly flowing with renewing power from the origin of all self-awareness.

I move my attention from false thoughts and move my attention to the unconditioned power that I am. I breathe easily. I relax in uniform consistency with the perfect pattern of intelligent power.

I surrender all limiting, constricting, deceptive thoughts on the altar of transformation. I turn these thoughts into pathways, doors, and passageways to higher conceptions of truth. In a higher place of truth, I dwell and allow all truth to form thoughts of wisdom that washes away all rigidity, blockage, and hardness from the instrument I call my physical body. I cleanse the total arrangement of my mind from all tension, constriction, and closures.

My mind is open, unobstructed, and directly connected to the one-mind. I feel my connection with the one-mind and openly receive new ideas, thoughts, concepts, and instructions that allow me to expand, grow, and transform the conditions of my world.

My attention moves automatically from conditioned thinking to unconditioned thinking. I can move my attention from mental conditions and therefore rearrange the conditions of my life. This process is simple, instant, and easy for me to do again and again. This is how I change my mental impressions, moods, and the events and circumstances that unfold as a result.

Confined - Exhale

I break free from all limiting thought and limiting habits of thought.

I am granted with serenity of mind and ease of being. I am at the center of my inner world and I am still, calm, and quiet in manner of expression.

Every part of my body-mind is perfectly patterned after the unity of the one-mind.

Even in diversity of expression I am one with all.

Even in perfect stillness, I accomplish all that is my good.

There is no confusion in oneness. There is no distortion in oneness. There is only perfect understanding and illumination in oneness. All is well.

The unfolding of my good reveals the majesty, creativity, and intelligence of the power of my being. I witness perfection unfolding in every manner of experience.

Through my imagination oriented and aligned in oneness perfection may come into form.

I have all that I need in mental faculties to attune to and express perfect ideas ever springing forth from the well that is the origin of all diversity.

I enter into every experience with gladness. I enter into every experience with the feeling of accomplishment for I know that every experience is an opportunity to experience oneness with all.

All good is available to me.

All that is good is available in one-mind because all is one and I am part and parcel with the one-mind.

Confinement - Liberty

I am at liberty. My mind is free to go to new places and free to experience new thoughts. When I free my attention and allow it to go to the places that are in store in the power of my being, I feel free and the instrument I call my physical body moves in harmony with the movement of liberated power.

I go where I am wanted and appreciated. I engage in activities that fulfill the expression of my desired mood. I am emotionally expansive and clear.

I liberate all that is my good from the confines of confined thinking. I liberate my mind from confined mental arrangements. I free myself and others from limited thinking.

I seek after liberty. I feel after it. I can know all expressions of liberty and find myself expanding to even greater levels of awareness. My experiences are new and acceptable to me. I feel good in my physical body as my mind feels calm and directed. I am oriented in the right direction of my good.

I experience positive interactions everywhere I go. Others feel at liberty with me. I feel at liberty with others. I set myself free to feel natural.

I liberate from the origin of all experiences even better experiences. I liberate from the origin of all material good even better material experiences. I liberate from the origin of oneness even greater experiences of oneness.

The power of my being is at liberty to create beauty, joy, and serenity into expression. I express my true self freely and abundantly.

Conflict - Cooperation

I feel my connection to the one-mind through everyone I meet.

I recognize the power, creativity, and mental faculties that we all share. I see that we are all capable of creating our experiences. I recognize the similarities we all share. I notice no differences. I recognize only unity and connection in oneness.

I recognize the origin of being in myself and in everyone I encounter in my experience. My experiences with all parties are always respectful, integritous, wholesome, and constructive.

I use my word in a manner that instills confidence in one's use of their creative faculties. My words are encouraging, helpful, illuminating, and liberating.

I am a helpful and gentle presence with a generous spirit that overflows with soothing thoughts and words.

Every part of me is in unison and cooperates entirely with all for the fulfillment of my good.

I share the wealth of truth in me freely and generously. I feel the power and presence of the one-mind in me, ever increasing my awareness of my distinct individuality. I feel the same for others. I recognize the distinctness in all.

My mind is aligned with the one-mind and directed by the voice of truth.

Every interaction I experience with others affirms this fact. I create goodness and beauty in every personal interaction.

I feel my connection to the family that is united in oneness.

I collaborate and communicate with all parties remembering the truth of who we are.

All is well.

All are one.

Confusion - Simplicity

All that is good is simple. All that is perfect is simple. All that is understood originates from simplicity.

Truth is simple. I recognize my simplicity. I understand who I am with fullness. I understand what I am capable of doing with my mental faculties.

My presence simplifies discordant conditions.

I organize and decipher all scrambled feelings, impressions, and conditions.

I decipher my moods and direct my attention and mental faculties in the improvement of my inner and outer experience.

My days are simple.

My experiences are clearly understood and simple.

My behaviors are simple.

My words are simple. I speak articulately.

I dissolve all conflict through cooperation. I can accomplish any goal with the committed fulfillment of simple tasks.

My world is simple because I am simple.

I think simply and thus what I produce is simplicity.

I make things easy because I am easy and in my ease I accomplish all.

The arrangement of my mind is in agreement with the one-mind.

I live truthfully. I speak truthfully. I behave truthfully.

Truth is my nature. Thus, my nature is simplicity.

Contorted - Poise

My mind is perfectly organized. My mind is free of false thought forms. I release false constructions from the total arrangement of my mind.

I turn to the power of my being, the origin of all poise and perfect thinking, to clarify my mind and the instrument I call my physical body.

I release years of calcified, rigid mental structures from my present experience.

I am known in oneness. The perfect image of my true mind and physical body enters into my imagination and into my attention.

I focus my attention on images of beauty, poise, perfection, and grace. In perfect movement of attention, I flow in harmony with the one-mind.

My physical body feels at ease. My physical body feels relaxed, strong, at ease, and unstoppable.

I am centered in the power of my being. I am carried by the power of my being.

I am moved by the power of my being. I am moved by the perfection of the one-mind.

I feel my connection to all. I feel embraced and uplifted by this ceaseless, everflowing connection.

Control - Trust

I am at ease. I go through every experience with ease of mind. I sense a deep feeling of rest in my being. I feel rested and calm in my body-mind. I always do what is best for me. For what is best for me always creates joy, peace, and serenity in my experience.

My heart is open to receive guidance, instruction, and steps aligned in truth. I take each step in acceptance of truth. I make decisions based on truth. I plant seeds of truth in my mind and accept their fruits in my experience.

I always have what I need because I am what I need. I am centered in well-being, steadiness, and joy. In harmony, I interact with others in my experience in such a manner that I notice expansion with every interaction.

I know that what is granted and assigned to me comes to me at the appointed opportunity. Every moment is an opportunity to express and experience my good. I surrender all false thoughts and assumptions by denying them my attention.

I orient my mind towards the truth of the one-mind.

I release all anguish for certainty.

I release all fear for serenity.

I release all frustration for progress.

I recapture the feeling of my power and sit, serenely in the presence of the one-mind in me. All is well in my inner world. Everything is complete in me. I am whole. I am united with the one-mind.

There is no limit to what the power of my being can accomplish. There is no limit to my ability to imagine. There is no limitation of experience. In my mind, I am free to explore, create, imagine, design anything of goodness. I am at ease and I am at rest.

There is no external mind. There is no external power. There is only oneness and oneness works perfectly to accomplish what I call into experience.

There is no sabotaging power or will that can undo my good or stop its fulfillment. There is no interfering power lest I turn my attention away from my good. The power of the one-mind is the only operative power and I retain my connection now and forever as I always have since the beginning.

I laugh in fulfillment. I smile in completion. I rest in wholeness. I act in wisdom. I am happiness experiencing itself.

Every word I say is based upon a loving thought. Every action is based upon a truth.

I trust in the power of my being.

The power of my being never fails, never abandons me, never betrays me.

The power of my being always delivers, is always present, and is always true.

Cramp - Flowing

I feel the circulating, unending, flowing presence of the one-mind moving through every channel of the instrument I call my physical body.

I feel the circulation of my presence of being going before me in all manner of experience, entering into all places designed for my good.

All obstructions dissolve from my mind. All mental patterns rooted in deception are obliterated immediately.

I can sense movement paced at the perfect pace. I can sense the power and presence of my being circulating and pulsating.

Every part of my physical body radiates with vitality.

I am at ease in my mind. I am at rest.

Every channel of my physical body and my mind is open so that all communication may flow.

I hear the communication of creative intelligence. I feel the direction and instruction of inspired movement.

I release all holds over my attention. I release my mind from all false mental habits of thought. There are no obstructive beliefs in my experience.

All is clear in my mind. All is stable and still in my experience.

I breathe fully. I breathe calmly.

Criticize - Observe

I observe all that enters into my awareness in an unconditioned presence of mind.

I am free from conditioned thinking. I release all conclusionary thinking. I release all false assumptions.

I observe my mental arrangement. I observe the mental arrangements of others with indifference. I release from my habit of mind all feelings of condemnation, contempt, hate, division, disgust, and loathing. I release all morbid thoughtforms that would have me distracted from the true, permanent sense of oneness that dwells in all.

I sense oneness in all spaces and dimensions. I feel the qualities of the one-mind expressing themselves through me. I am enthralled by the beauty, unity, and everlasting diversity of the one-mind that expresses its qualities through me and all.

I observe the completion of all good. I observe the perfection of every complete, accomplished state of expression in all forms at all times.

I observe events as they occur with the power of my power of being. I observe the greater fulfillment of good despite the appearances of false conditions. I observe and recognize my true nature in myself and all distinct self-aware parts of the one-mind.

I observe my actions with full understanding. I observe the actions of all distinct self-aware parts of the one-mind with full understanding. I observe oneness in full attention.

Cry - Communicate

I am attuned to the communication of truth. Truth seeks expression through me and I open the doorways so that truth may enter into my experience.

I understand the communication of the instrument I call my physical body. I understand the communication that enters into my mind through symbols, images, thoughts, words, and concepts.

I intuitively understand communication of all kinds. I understand unspoken and spoken communication.

I see the communication of patterns around me.

I immediately understand what I see and hear.

I synthesize any type of communication into a clear, distinct message.

I understand the communication of my body. I understand how my body communicates instructions for the fulfillment of vitality and radiance.

I clearly communicate messages of truth and deliver ideas directly. I know what to do with communication and to whom I must deliver communication. I receive communication effortlessly and integrate knowledge to my immediate benefit.

I know how to communicate with my power.

I know how to direct my power to fulfill the outcomes of my decisions. My power understands my decisions and fulfills them immediately.

D
Damaged - Integrity

No experience, image, thought, or temporary condition may erode my integrity.

I am whole. I was always whole. I will always be whole.

In every shape, form, and experience I am whole.

The instrument I call my physical body is whole. Every aspect of my mind is whole and perfect and complete.

I release all damaging patterns of thought. I release all contorting thoughts.

I release all images of destruction, disease, and morbidity.

I am poised. I am vital. I am organized.

The power of my being, the perfect essence of oneness, is integritous.

I act in integrity. I am moved by the intelligence of the one-mind.

I act according to my true nature as formless, shapeless awareness as the life giving force of the one-mind.

I see myself as I am in my natural state of being. I move as I move in my natural state of being. I feel as I feel in my natural state of being.

The total arrangement of my mind and the instrument I call my physical body is the perfect image of oneness.

Danger - Security

I feel the perfect stillness of my being.

My mind is perfectly still and focused on the harmony of oneness.

All deceptive thoughts leave the realm of my mind immediately and permanently.

I see the perfection of the one-mind. I recognize with my sensing faculties the organization of creative, intelligent power.

All illusions of false thinking depart my attention revealing my natural mental clarity.

My good is guaranteed. I am endowed with the power that is truth.

I exercise my decision making capacities to orient my attention firmly towards the power of my being to receive the inherent goodness of the one-mind that is flowing in me and through me.

My inner world is calm. My inner world is serene and perfectly arranged to reflect the perfection that is the one-mind.

I deny all illusions of external power. I deny all illusions of a separate mind.

I release my attention from all experiences rooted in deception.

I orient myself towards freedom, liberty of experience, serenity and oneness. I am immediately directed and moved by the intelligent awareness of security.

All is well in my world.

All is still in my world.

I am free.

Death - Birth

I enter into oneness with the original of all. I feel my place as an essential, integral part of the whole. I am precious, important, valuable, and essential to the origin of all distinction. I see and recognize my place amongst all.

There is no division, no separation, no otherness. I enter into the world of experience to remember this fundamental truth that all are one. I feel the pulsation of the one-mind in my heart beat. My breath is the evidence of the never ending movement of oneness that connects us all.

Water symbolizes the connection we all share. Earth symbolizes the world of form that is animated by the life-giving force of presence. The sun symbolizes the light inherent in us all because I am intelligent light. I am intelligent light moving through infinite forms. I am a presence experiencing my distinct mental arrangements.

I constantly change forms. I am always moving and rearranging my mind.

I am not the arrangement of my mind. I am not the instrument I call my physical body. I am not the activities in which I engage my mind and apply the power of my being.

I am life giving force and enter into any form to glorify the everlasting truth of oneness expressing itself through a diversity of forms.

I release all attachment to external conditions. I release all attachment to mental forms and habits of thinking. I enter into new experiences fully aware of my true nature. I feel free, liberated, and at peace.

I expand the power of my being to experience ever greater vistas of self-understanding.

I am fulfilled in all ways. I am expressed in all ways. All is well because all is one.

There is no enemy in my mind. There is no otherness. There is only oneness. All are one.

I accept the gifts available to me through the everlasting endowment of my connection to the origin of all creative thought. I feel the goodness of my being and content in the fullness of my being.

I am vital. I am pure. I am calm and serene.

I see clearly, feel accurately, and sense with perfect understanding.

I am ready to experience all forms of expression. I am ready to explore all places in one-mind. I accept truth in all forms. I integrate truth in all forms into my experience.

Debt - Enough

I am always enough. I am aware of my fullness of mind. I am aware of my fullness of presence. My attention is connected to the one-mind and is thus connected to all self-aware parties. Through this connection, I am able to access the thoughts, concepts, and images necessary to grow in understanding that inspires intelligent action.

All of my experiences always start with me. What I say about myself determines my experience. Thus, I always speak greatly of who I am, my capacities, my capabilities, and my potential.

I am always enough to fulfill my good in every possible way; whether by connecting with other minds, creating imaginal designs, speaking and affirming my good, and acting in an intelligent manner.

I have enough to start with. I have enough to continue. I have enough to finish the fulfillment of my good.

Where I am is enough to create a new world. The intelligent use of my mind is enough to begin the transformation of my world.

I can always start again and renew my mind and therefore my world.

I craft my world with my words. I use my words constructively and use my words intelligently. I see, hear, and understand clearly. I speak confidently about myself and my power. I know what I am capable of achieving by the constructive use of my power.

Deceived - Discover

Every experience ultimately increases my knowledge of the truth that all is one in one-mind.

Every thought that enters into my awareness tells me its original source. I can easily discern the difference between a truthful thought and a false thought. I can recognize true forms of thought and false thoughtforms.

I am always aware of the truth. I always act upon the truth and allow truth to unveil itself in my experiences.

As patterns unfold into my outer world, I intelligently discern true ideas from false ideas. I create imaginal designs based on truth and dissolve and neutralize false conditions.

With the faculty of my attention and through the active engagement of my imagination, I discover all manner of experiences and accept them into my inner world.

I am always growing in awareness of greater vistas of truth. I am able to understand more, do more with my body-mind, and fabricate new experiences.

I am always doing something new. I am always breaking past old patterns of thought. I am ever expanding in discovery of my true identity and as a result exercise my true capacities.

Confidently, I enter into new experiences aware of my intentions. I pierce the illusions in my inner and outer world. I dissolve all manner of false conditions. I am free from deceptive and limiting thinking. I am magnanimous in presence and unstoppable in movement.

Truth is my guide. The voice of the one-mind speaks clear instructions to my ear.

Visions of beauty, truth, and perfection delight my imagination. I feel a serene altitude of mind. I feel impervious to distraction. I feel sheltered and protected by an air of silence.

Good is always at work in my world. Good is always accomplished in my world.

Defeated - Victorious

I am victorious because I do not interrupt the creative power of my being with falsities and deceptions.

I do not divert my power towards the creation of false thoughtforms and behaviors that would create mixed results.

The results I get are based upon the continuous, steady stream of my attention on the fulfillment of my good.

Undistracted, I focus my creative propensities on the creation of good in my experience. I give myself only to moods that embody the good that I deem acceptable to create.

I create lovely images in my imagination. I harness my concentrated attention for the betterment of all.

I starve out false thinking by repeating to myself the truth of my salvation.

I turn my attention to the results I desire to achieve and affirm them with my word. I feel the completion of my word in me. I feel its fulfillment in my inner experience and I express that fulfillment through my choices, actions, and habits.

I am unwavering in my commitment to the fulfillment of good in me. I do not wane in the powerful, unrelenting connection to the origin of all power and the everlasting, renewing organizing power of the one-mind.

I rest solidly on the foundation of positive thinking.

I remain true by the installment of habits that fulfill my good. I dedicate my attention and my world in reservation to the truth that is available to me.

I will not be deceived by divisive thinking. I abide in the unity of the one-mind and stay true to the connection that I share with all. Through this connection I am victorious.

Defend - Unimpeachable

The power of my being is an unimpeachable fortress.

The only thoughts that may enter my mind are truthful thoughts. No false thoughts may enter into my attention, nor may be accepted by me. All attempts at distraction, deception, or attack automatically fail.

I stand poised, strengthened by the integrity of my being and the sheer power of my presence. My presence of mind is unshakeable and unbreachable. The joy of my being is impenetrable.

All false images directed towards me are immediately returned to their sender so they may learn the truth of their actions.

I reject all false thoughts. I only accept good thoughts aligned with unity and intelligent awareness.

I am whole, secure, and serene. I know my inherent worth and am integritous in all my doing. I only engage my mind and creative activity in the fulfillment of goodness in my experience.

I create mental images of myself that are whole, honest, and empowering.

I understand and appreciate my nature.

Others see me truthfully and speak only good of me as I see others truthfully and see only good of them.

I have faith in my true self, my potential, and identity as a unified part of the one-mind.

There is only the unity of the one-mind.

Deferred - Immediate

My dreams are immediately available to me now.

I immediately have and experience my good now. There is no need to wait, for I experience my dreams to their fullest now.

As I become aware of what is available in me, I enter into that eternal and internal experience in the power of my being through the faculty of my imagination.

I explore my dreams. I experience my dreams through my imaginative senses. I immediately expand them into my physical reality as their impulses become ideas, instructions, and guidance that enters into my inner world. They direct me to the path of my dream's fulfillment in my outer world.

In my world, my dreams are always possible. My dreams exist in me and come through me.

The more I enter into my dream, the more immediate and imminent it feels.

Through my desire to fully experience my dreams in my world, I enter into them through my imagination. As I experience my dreams inside my imagination, I feel the impressions starting to take hold of my attention. I immediately see my dream in its fulfilled state. I see the scene of its fulfillment in fullness of sensation. I see it, hear it, feel it, taste it, touch it in my imagination. I feel now - immediately - the satisfaction of its completion and fullness of expression. I immediately create an experience in my imagination and enter into the fullness of a desired experience.

All desired states exist in me.

I feel my connection to the origin of all pleasant experiences and find every possible dream there.

My dreams first start off as subtle impressions. With my focused attention, I magnify my dreams until they become larger, more real, and stimulate in me more impressions. Immediately, I know the answers to my questions.

Immediately, I know the plans for their expression.

Immediately, I know the hour of its fulfillment. Because the plans for my dream's fulfillment are complete, I know there is nothing I must do but to enter into the experience in my imagination and allow my dream to enter into my world.

I forget all concepts of delay.

I release all false assumptions that would have me believe that my dreams are far off and away. The truth is, my dreams are immediately available to me now.

My resources are immediately available to me now. Help and support are immediately available to me now. The answers and solutions are immediately available to me now. Ideas and instructions are immediately available to me now. Clarity of mind is available to me now.

Deficient - Enumerated

I am enumerated. I am one with money. I am connected to the origin of all money. I see great amounts of money in my experiences and at my command.

I associate myself with an ever increasing store of money. Money, in great stores, is available and accessible by me.

I know money in my mind. I experience money in a constructive way.

I multiply money mentally, automatically, and intuitively in exponential amounts.

My stores of money multiply naturally. Each environment where I place my money multiplies it everlastingly. The money in my stores continues for generations.

The amount of money that I claim is ever multiplying.

I am sheltered in mind. I am my own economy. I am my own bank. I am financially established in my own mind as an ever growing success. I am unshakeable as I have constructed in my mind a foundation of monetary stability.

I think only of the immediate power of creation and how I only dwell upon thoughts of growing monetary strength. The money I know in my mind is expansive. The power of my being overpowers any thoughts of lack or insecurity.

It is my business to observe and steward money to grow. I nurture the money in my care and place it in conditions where it will surely multiply.

My money works for me night and day. My money increases night and day. I see opportunities to grow my wealth and know exactly what to do to allow it to grow.

There is nothing in my mind but thoughts of increasing the supply of money. It is easy for me to see monetary potential and to seize it immediately.

Money is a thoughtform. I increase the thoughtform of money in my mind by appointing my power to magnify it. The power in me gives my money growth.

The money I have in mind is a reality that I enjoy and use. I have an ever increasing appreciation of money and explore the wisdom of stewarding money for good.

I look to the origin of money to experience money. I experience money in my mind and understand it perfectly. I understand money and how to steward it.

Money is easy for me to conceive of. I release all thoughts inconsistent with money. I release all moods inconsistent with growing money. I release all decisions that have repelled money from me. I gravitate money into my experience. Experiences come together for me in which I may behold money.

The amount of money with which I associate my name is enumerated by me in my mind. I decide the amount of money in the accounts that bear my name. I decide the amount of money that is in my use.

Delirious - Clarified

I am clarified. I am the clear flowing light. I am pure, uniform, expanding light.

My mind is clear and free. The physical instrument I call my body is clean, boundless, and unrestricted. Every part of my body-mind functions harmoniously with the thoughts of the one-mind.

My world is clear, bright, and open. I am the light of the one-mind shining into my world and I move effortlessly throughout my world. I breathe steadily, calmly everywhere in my entire mind and physical body.

The organ I call my heart is the vessel through which the power that I am vibrates into the instrument I call my physical body and gives a pattern to the development of my body.

Thus, my physical body goes where my power directs it to go. My brain organizes the functions of my body according to the instructions I give it through the assumptions I allow to dwell in my mind. And so, I only allow truth to dwell in my mind and clarify with the light of truth all false thoughts, shadows, and belief in an external power and separation from the one-mind.

All tension disperses from my body. What was closed is open. What was pinched is filled. Where there was pain there exists comfort.

All illusions and delusions are swept away and I am clarified in the presence of the eternal, magnificent power of the one-mind.

I am reminded of every joy in my life. I can distinctly remember every instance of connection I felt with all parts of the one-mind - all animated, self-aware presences. I am rejuvenated and revitalized with the memory of every fulfilled promise.

I delight in imagining even more grandeur, beauty, joy, and connection there is to come.

I am appreciated, recognized, and valued without end or limit. I feel that appreciation directed towards me and I direct this truth into my world to all.

I receive ideas and concepts of health, prosperity, and success. I have so much to experience, so much good to know.

Delusion - Silence

I am centered, still, and calm. I am the power that calms the arrangement of my mind. I center thoughts and freeze them in my mind. I can easily pause a thought and cause it to freeze in my mind. I can observe the thought slowly. I can see all angles of a thought and notice its details in calm detachment. I can objectively observe any thought without accepting it into the temple of my inner world. I instantly know the consequences of a thought and either choose to accept or reject its pattern.

I recognize thoughts clearly with understanding and knowing. I recognize all parties and their thoughts clearly with understanding and knowing. I distinguish where my world ends and another's world begins. I easily recognize the creations of my imagination and how they manifest in my experience.

Every part of my being is soft, circulating, flowing, and open. My body-mind is rested and at ease.

I am vitality experiencing itself. I feel rejuvenating power clarifying my mind and organizing imaginal designs to embody truth.

I am expansive power of being. I am in harmony with the entirety of the one-mind. I use the instrument I call my physical body correctly. I am poised. I am aligned only with the truth that emanates from the one-mind.

My heart beats calmly to the pulsation of the one-mind. I feel new, organized thoughts entering into my awareness showing me the grandeur and limitless oneness that emanates through the connection I share with all in one-mind.

The power of my being is ageless, infinite, limitless, boundaryless, and ever loving. Every part of me is good. I accept every part of me. I ignore all thoughts of lack, hatred, destruction, and impurity. I deny all false conditions. I renounce all delusions of thought. My mind is intently and permanently connected to the everlasting truth of the one-mind. All I do is motivated by truth. All of my decisions are rooted in ever expanding vistas of truth. I see clearly, feel goodness, and immediately know my good.

Every experience is a gift. Every experience is an opportunity granted to me through the origin of all awareness. I revel in the joy of being. I feel the endowment of all creation. I feel a wealth of all positive thoughts. I receive beautiful thought forms into my awareness and give them life in my experience.

I am one with all. All is one with me. All is one.

Denial - Pledge

I pledge myself to the promise I intend to fulfill. I am committed to my vision. I ignore contrary thoughts to my vision.

I deny my attention to doubtful thoughts which are merely false thoughtforms contrary to my promise of fulfillment. I recognize doubtful thoughts for what they are: a false imaginal design that is a shadow of our present limited perception of conditions.

I pledge myself to my vision. I pledge my attention only to my expected dream. I heed no other observation. I deny current conditions as the determiner of my experience.

I guarantee myself to my vision and to no other imaginal design. I guard my imaginal designs with determination. I regard my imaginational designs as completed fact. My imaginational designs are accepted and certain to realize in my experience.

I assert myself to no other version of events. I pledge attention only to those experiences that fulfill my good. I withdraw my attention from all other experiences that do not align with my expected dream.

I know that the power of my being creates my experiences. I only pledge the power of being to create good experiences.

Deny - Believe

I accept truth in all forms to enter into my mind.

I accept truth as the operative pattern by which I base all of my thoughts, words, and actions.

Truth is the guiding principle in my experience. I act on truth and make decisions based on truth.

I accept myself as a self-aware part of the one-mind, the source of all experience, oneness, and truth. Truth contains all relief, solutions, opportunities, and knowledge that liberates me from false attitudes and self-deceptions.

I accept my power to create and uncreate. I accept my power to give life to my imaginal designs. I accept goodness in all forms in my experience. I accept love - the active sharing of truth - of all forms. I integrate truth into my mind.

I release, reject, and dissolve all false thoughts from my mind. I use the instrument I call my physical body as the pattern generator of truth. My body is an outpicturing of beautiful, honest thoughts in my inner world.

My outer world is the stage upon which I express truth aware to me in my inner world. I have authority and governance over my experience regardless of outer conditions. I can see my path of fulfillment. I am aware of and motivated by the truth that liberates all from deceptive illusions. No condition, illusion, false thoughtform can contain me and prevent me from fulfilling my good.

I am the mind that embodies truth and creates it in my experience. What I accept is what I embody. What I embody is what I bring forth into my experience. What I experience is a testament to the truths that I accept into my mind.

Dependent - Self-Existent

I am self-existent. I give myself all things with a thought. I am powerfully creative and I generate anything in my imagination by thinking intently on it. Everything comes from the origin of all supply and all comes through oneness in the most ingenious ways. We are all able to supply ourselves through this faculty of mind.

Because I am self-existent, I forget all false assumptions that my good only comes from specific people, institutions, or places. All supply comes from the origin of all experience. I place my trust, faith, and attention in direct connection with the true source.

Because I am self-existent, I need nothing. I want nothing. I have it all within the creative power that I am. All is given and granted in one mind. I remember that I am an inheritor of all desirable experiences. I release all holds on my attention, thereby releasing all holds on my good. I experience my good now and know that I am fully endowed.

I embody vitality, wealth, serenity, joy, and capacity to imagine and experience all good. I free my attention to fully experience all the good that the joy of being has to offer. I appropriate good feelings and experience them immediately.

No barrier exists between me and my good. I focus my power of my being and attention on my unique ideas and go into the place where these ideas dwell. I first experience them in my imagination until I am satisfied. I move my attention, energy, and power - all one and the same - into the new experience and there I dwell.

I always have what is required immediately available to me for each experience. I am fully prepared and equipped for every experience. I have a storehouse available in the power of my being. I know what to do and where to go in every experience. I move gracefully and steadily through every experience.

Deplete - Neutral

My state of being is neutral.

The arrangement of my mind is in balance with the one-mind. In a position of neutrality, I am perfectly poised. I am correctly positioned. I am stable, centered, and whole.

The arrangement of my mind is neutral. The power inherent in me neutralizes all false feelings. I radiate neutralizing warmth, vitality, and rejuvenation through my entire body-mind.

I feel unconditioned. I feel peaceful and serene.

My attention is solely aligned with the radiating presence of the one-mind in my entire experience.

Neutrality radiates into my world and neutralizes all false conditions.

All chaotic patterns are dissolved.

All destructive patterns vanish in the light of the one-mind.

The instrument I call my body is empowered, full of light, emanating with consistent, everlasting life.

I rest in the living presence of the one-mind that is my true being.

I restore my mind from all false impressions into a neutral state.

My mind is quiet, serene, and calm.

I feel quietness, serenity, and calmness.

Deprived - Endowed

I am endowed. I have everything I imagine.

I feel all that is my good now. I have me and within me is the origin of all experience. I experience all that my attention is aligned with in my imagination. I clearly see in my imagination the experiences that are enjoyable to me.

I gravitate my attention to everything that is pleasurable, enjoyable, and delightful. I am in this moment and, going forward, continually supported, financed, endowed with the resources that I require to accomplish my good.

I live with purpose and all that is required to fulfill my purpose calls me and I answer.

I give freely, wisely, and graciously. I receive freely, wisely, and graciously.

I am endowed with so much good and joy in me that I can feel it flowing abundantly through me and around me. The oneness endowed in me flows freely and goes to those individuals, creations, and places where it can do the most good. I am received with appreciation, gratitude, and warmth.

I laugh freely and I express myself freely. I am aware of who I am in the purest essence. The experiences I create for myself are loving, pleasurable, and serene.

Wherever I go I am welcomed, because the good I send out summons me to meet it. I gravitate to others who are aware of their own endowment and I bless my feelings of endowment to those who are awakening to their good.

My cup of life always runs over and blesses those around me. I share because I know there is always enough. Goodness never stops coming into my experience and I am delighted by the gifts that come to me each new day. I continue to give of my good first in my own thoughts and feelings and then spread into my experiences.

I am endowed with what is required to fulfill my projects. I have access to my endowment now. I can use it, distribute it, and employ it for my good. All of my projects are generously funded by my endowment. Money, resources, manpower, and ideas come together efficiently and quickly.

The right people enter into my experience to collaborate with me on the fulfillment of a shared good. We enjoy each other's company, expertise, and collaborate together in harmony.

Financial resources are plenty. I know where to access financial means to fulfill my dreams. Money comes to me before I even realize I need it. With every step I take, I am greeted with the ideas, tools, and resources that construct my good.

I am recognized in the one mind. My dreams and goals are recognized and fulfilled in the one mind. My dreams and goals *come* from the one mind. I originate in one mind. Perfect arrangement comes from the one mind. Everything is accomplished in one mind.

I am one with all. I am one with my good. I am aware of my good and its completion. I imagine my good in its completion. The origin of dreams is the first cause. My experience is the effect. I am the inheritor of all dreams. They are fulfilled through me and my oneness with all.

I can think of nothing but my dreams. My dreams contain their instructions. The more I focus my attention on my dreams, the more I am aware of their fulfillment. I trust my dreams to provide me with the steps to take. I do not have to wait. The steps are available to me now. I delight in the awareness of my dreams and their instructions. I fulfill them in peace and satisfaction.

Despair - Rejoice

Every part of me rejoices for my existence.

I feel the laughter of unadulterated pleasure of living.

I feel the fortune of my being. I am free, aware, liberated part of the whole.

My entire world rejoices. I rejoice.

I am happiness incarnate.

I feel my own happiness. I exude and express happiness in all its forms.

I rejoice in celebration of my self-awareness and the ability to create with my imaginative faculties in the expression of my unity with the whole.

I rejoice in the fulfillment of every beautiful thought.

I rejoice in the recognition of other distinct self-aware parts of the one-mind.

I respect all as I respect myself because we all share a connection to each other as a united whole. All are one.

I rejoice in every moment. I rejoice with every movement. I dance, laugh, play, smile, and go through every experience with ease.

I rejoice because I get to be myself everywhere I go and with everyone I meet. I rejoice with every new opportunity to be one with all.

Destroy - Coexist

Every self-aware, distinct part of the one-mind exists totally and completely within the one-mind.

We can never be separated and we are never separated.

Only seeing a shadow of the false thought that we may be separated is the farthest we can perceptually be from the origin of all and from each other.

The fact was and remains that we are part and parcel of the one-mind.

Together, everyone co-exists in the one-mind in our own individual self-aware experience.

We are never separated. We are only distinct.

The only means by which I may be separated from any party is through awareness.

I may move my attention to any place within the one-mind. I am not the images I express in the world of form. I cannot be destroyed. I can only move my presence from the world of form and into the other realms available to me in the one-mind.

Nothing is ever destroyed. Through our connection to the one-mind and our existence in one-mind we can feel for each other and immediately recognize each other's presence.

Wherever we may be, we can also be aware of our connection and inherent existence in a shared mind.

I coexist with all distinct parts of the one-mind.

I can create in my experience and positively benefit others who exist in their own experience.

I am one with all. All is one.

Destructive - Improving

My world is ever improving because I am in it. I use my imagination to create imaginative designs that always improve those conditions patterned after deceptive thinking. I can improve anything that can benefit from a transformation.

I am endowed with the operative power of all transformation. I move conditions with the movements of my attention. I turn my attention to the source of all ideas and feel my connection to the source and draw out an idea that is sure to improve conditions around me.

My awareness focuses more and more on beautiful concepts to the point that the only thoughts that enter into my mind are beautiful, stable, and restorative.

I am a restorative presence. When I enter into an environment, I begin immediately improving where I am with the light of my being. The power of my being illuminates all dark places. The power of my being beautifies all false conditions. I am beautiful and bring beauty with me. I am transformative and bring transformation with me. I am illuminated and thus cast light into my world.

I stay true to the origin of my being. I abstain from conditioning my mind to other people's moods. I only condition my mind upon truth and everlasting goodness of the origin of all being. Wherever I dwell, I increase in understanding of this eternal connection to and oneness with the one-mind.

Because I am oriented towards and aligned with the one-mind, this power enters into any experience and improves it immediately.

Everything gets better wherever I go. Everyone feels better wherever I go.

I always leave conditions better than when I first encountered them. The perfection of my being creates perfection and I allow the pattern of perfection to emanate through the arrangement of my mind.

Detached - Embodied

I am embodied by the creative, intelligent, aware, perceptive power of the one-mind. With this embodiment, I am able to do all things, understand all things, and fulfill all good.

There is no other mind or power that lives and dwells in the instrument I call my physical body. There is no other voice I hear. There is no other presence that I feel.

The one-mind meets my attention through all parties. The one-mind shows me how appreciated, valued, esteemed, and distinguished I am through all parties.

The power of my being is the truth that I experience and express at all times. There are infinite ways to express this creative intelligence and infinite ways to partner with this power in my imagination.

I am the embodiment of good. I am the embodiment of truth. I am the embodiment of peace. I am the embodiment of stability, centeredness, and care.

I feel the goodness of my being and experience it in my inner and outer worlds. I am present in the moment and centered where I ever observe myself to be.

I am oriented in one-mind. My steps and my days are directed with clear instructions and wise guidance. The power and presence of the one-mind goes with me, is me, ever expansive and ever present. I am heard, acknowledged, and answered at all times and in all experiences.

In the power of my being I am endowed, granted, and inherently given all manner of good. I naturally, easily, and wondrously express my good and experience it immediately in my inner and outer worlds.

Everything is simple in one-mind. Everything is clear, understood, and facile. I am the embodiment of simplicity.

Difficult - Natural

I am natural. I am made from the origin of being. I am natural because I am self-aware intelligence. Everything I am composed of is natural. Because I am natural everything about me is pure, perfect, and organized.

I act naturally. I act according to my nature. My nature is creative, productive, and eternal power. I am a life giving force.

I think about the result I select and I naturally experience it with my imaginative faculty. Results occur naturally for me because results flow from me. Naturally occurring results come as an effect of the visions I hold in my imagination. I feel natural experiencing the effects of my imaginative designs. Every experience in the physical extension of my mind is natural.

I accomplish that which I decide to accomplish with ease and naturalness of being. Every activity I engage my awareness in is natural for me. Everything I do is natural. What is natural is good. Goodness is natural. I am good and I am natural. I am natural at what I do.

My interactions are natural. Because my interactions are natural, they are effortless. My experiences are natural because they come from me, a natural power. With my presence, I enter situations and create a recognition of naturalness.

My growth is natural. My progress is natural. My mind is natural. My expansion is natural. My thoughts are natural. My moods are natural. I am at ease in my environment. I am in nature with my environment and my environment is in nature with me. I am in harmony with my environment and those in my environs.

I conduct myself in an easy, natural fashion. I speak naturally. I behave naturally.

Disagree - Harmony

I am harmony. Harmony fills my mind and enters into my experience. My mental environment is harmonious and thus the power of my being reflects that in my world.

My world shows me what I imagine. My world shows me what I believe my power is capable of doing. My world shows me all that I assume is true of others and my nature.

My world is in harmony with me. I am in harmony with the origin of all truth. Truth provides all perfect thoughts that shape my world.

Truth provides me with ideas, concepts, and thoughtforms that are beautiful, good, and strong. As a result, my world reflects the one-mind.

Every part of my own distinct self-awareness reflects the origin of truth.

I discipline my attention solely to focus on truth. As a result, I think truthfully, speak truthfully, and behave in a manner that is akin to perfection.

Every individual I meet is in harmony with what they give their attention to. As a result, their experiences are a mirror image of their imaginal designs. I dismantle every false image in my mind and dwell on thoughts that are acceptable to me.

Disappointed - Promised

I am the fulfillment of the promise. The promise is to express and experience as my origin. I am the originator of my experiences.

I am the decision maker in my imagination. I am the inheritor of joy, liberty, peace, exuberance, and creativity. These feelings and more are available to me to create my reality like colors to a canvas.

The process of creation never fails because I am the animating force through which creation is possible. Even when I was not aware of this fact, it was and is so.

I am aware of my true nature, what I can do by using my natural faculties, and everything that is available to me. That is the promise.

I accept only those thoughts that are acceptable to me. I only give life to that which is good. When I recognize a good idea, I accept it into the temple of my inner being. It enters in and I feel it with my imaginal senses until I have implanted the idea in the womb of my being.

As the co-creator with the origin, I always feel supported, surrounded, and whole.

I am known in one-mind, a part and parcel of the whole, connected to the origin and all other self-aware parts of the whole. Because of this unity, honesty is available to everyone to know, to co-create with, and experience.

I live my life truthfully. I create truthful experiences. This is how I awaken the connection I share with everyone I meet and encounter and beauty, friendship, and constructive experiences. I can not be disappointed when I think and live truthfully. The fruit of the experiences I create are truthful as I am aligned with the truth of my being.

Discouraged - Sure

I am sure. I know that my good is assured and certain to occur. I am guaranteed progress. I am guaranteed my good. I see with sureness of mind the effects of my thoughts occurring as I see them in my mind.

With sureness of mind, I see no other thoughts other than that which I have decided to experience. I stay focused on thoughts that I have decided are suitable for me. I only think of what is suitable for me.

I feel satisfied with my decisions. I know, when I make a decision, all the elements required to fulfill my decision immediately come together. Sureness guarantees the fulfillment of my good. Sureness determines the direction I go. I am sure of mind. I am sure the effects of my thoughts come into experience.

With sureness, I rest my mind.

With sureness, I am calm and still.

With sureness, I see all with a steady determination. With sureness, I trust and allow the forces of the one mind to arrange my mind into perfect form. My desires are fulfilled. I will not allow any other alternative experience to occur.

There is no other experience for me besides the experience I have chosen. I live each day easily and pleasantly. I focus my attention only on my good. My good is mine, guaranteed to me by the power of my being. Nobody determines my experiences but me.

I have the source of all my dreams within me. Because of this fact, all experiences flow from this origin, through me.

There is nothing but mind. All is mind. What is in my mind is my experience. I select my creative mental designs with precision. My creative mental designs are beautiful, harmonious, and peaceful. I design my experiences and because of this fact, I am sure that I will experience my designs in their apportioned moment.

I feel time. I see events. I know their purpose. I am the designer of my experiences. I am free to choose my experiences. I am sure that my chosen experiences will occur at the correct time. The correct time is when I am prepared for my designs. For, I prepare my mind with a mental arrangement of readiness.

When I feel ready for my design to come into experience, I enter into the scene. I enter into the scene in my imagination and practice my role until I feel prepared to receive my good.

I am sure of this process. I am assured of the outcomes I mentally construct in my imagination. This process never fails me because I cannot fail. I am sure.

Disease - Perfection

Perfection is my natural state of being. Perfection is my natural psychological state.

Perfectly was how I originated as a distinct, self-aware part and parcel of the one-mind.

I see the best version of me in my imagination. I see the best version of all that I encounter. I see the best of everything in my experience and I see past all false conditions and temporary, fleeting thoughtforms.

I see progress in all activities. I see growth in all areas of my mind. I see my thoughts evolving in greater harmony with the one-mind.

My feelings touch perfection. I feel the pattern, shape, and form of perfection, and through me the pattern of perfection is amplified through my mind and the instrument I call my physical body.

I direct my attention to thoughts originating from the one-mind. I direct my mood to express happiness, peace, health, and wholeness.

My physical body reflects the perfect pattern of vitality. Each day, my body-mind is revitalized by the pure power of my being. Each day, I awaken refreshed, full of power ready to experience the fulfillment of my good.

I am creative intelligence aware of myself. I am impervious to false impressions. I am greater than all temporary conditions. The magnanimity of the power in me neutralizes all false thoughts and morbid patterns.

I feel the reinvigoration of my body-mind at all times.

I am poised. I use my mind-body in a perfectly correct fashion in complete alignment with the one-mind.

I feel good because I feel the goodness that is inherent in me.

All is well in my mind. All is calm in my world.

Disparaged - Distinguished

I feel important and distinguished. My presence satisfies all needs. My mind is secure and calm. I see myself with feelings of honor, grace, and poise.

The only opinion that is valuable to me is my own. I hold myself in the highest regard just as I hold others in high regard. I expect others to respect me as I respect myself.

The only voice I hear in my mind is the power of my being. I listen to the power of my being. My voice as my voice imitates the voice of the origin of all truth.

I know that I am important because the origin of all being thought uniquely of me. I value myself exceedingly and importantly because I am original. My existence is essential.

I am equally distinguished amongst us all and all creation. I have my own unique flair, personality, and means of experience.

My contribution is valued by the origin of all life that exists everywhere, in everyone, and animates all forms.

I see through the moods of others and know the truth.

I do not hear, believe, or accept deceptions. I only listen for and receive truth.

Illusions dissolve and fade away as I focus my attention on clear thinking and action.

I am a free thinker and I dwell on freedom.

Dispassionate - Interested

I am interested and engaged.

What I give my attention to grows bigger and bigger in my experience. Connecting my attention, thereby opening my connection to the origin of all transformation, immediately corrects all undesirable forms or experiences making it good.

Turning my attention to the truth reveals my natural beauty, harmony, and serenity in my experience which becomes more enhanced as thoughts flow from this source.

I am interested in bringing joy, exhilaration, and contentment in every experience. I create beauty, peace, and companionship with the origin of intelligent presence. I am free to express my distinctness and am fully fulfilled in expression.

I smile at the world and the world smiles back at me. The joy I create in my inner world is evidenced by my experiences. Everywhere I direct my attention creates harmony.

The interest I direct into an idea grows my understanding and therefore wisdom of that which I focus my attention on. I sense my unification with the origin of all, I feel sheltered, secure, stable, and calm. I know that I can accomplish the fulfillment of all good acts in peace.

I feel good about everything I do. I feel good from everything I think because my mind is oriented towards the origin of all good.

All false thoughts are destroyed by the transformative power of truth. I seek truth and truth saves me from all false sensations.

I am creative simply by turning my attention to an idea and implanting it in the womb of my inner being. By entering an idea into my imagination, I animate it with movement and expansion.

What is good interests me. What is good illuminates me. What is good appreciates me. What is good finds my attention and directs my power.

I am united with what is good. I am good.

Disregarded - Revered

I am revered by all in my world. All are aware of my presence and my activities. All embrace me and value my activities. I am recognized as important, integral, and valuable to society.

I am highly revered and respected for my contributions to my community. I am known for my contributions and for my thinking. I feel invited to be myself and to express myself in the presence of all. Being myself and expressing myself improves all the places I enter into. I make a positive difference in the lives of all in my world. Everyone from all walks of life respects and values me just as I respect and value everyone from all walks of life.

I am revered for how I use my talents. I am revered for how I use my mind. I am revered for the positive effects of my moods. I am included in my community for the valuable benefit of my positive mind. My contributions are revered as important and helpful. My words are respected, honored, and used to create more good in the experiences of all.

My creations are revered as useful, helpful, and important in the experiences of all. I hold an important position in the experiences of all as a positive mind. People talk about my presence with reverence. People think of my presence with reverence. People talk of my contributions with reverence. People remember my presence with reverence. I am revered.

Distracted - Efficient

I am efficient. My activities are organized efficiently. Everything I do is efficient. I think efficient thoughts. I get efficient ideas.

My resources work efficiently for me. My operations run efficiently. I always profit from my efforts and gain from my investments.

My mind is focused on important tasks and goals for today. I leave other tasks to others who can manage them efficiently. I have enough time to do everything I need to do today.

The one mind resolves all seemingly unresolved matters. All my matters are resolved perfectly. All the world's matters are resolved peacefully and harmoniously.

I know where my responsibility begins and ends. I know where other's responsibilities begin and end.

I am on track and accomplish my good in due time.

The right parties and resources come to participate in the resolution of all matters. I feel supported and encouraged by those around me.

Distraught - Unshakeable

I am unshakeable. I am immovable. I am impervious to false conditions. I am immune to all false impressions.

I am immutable. I am everlasting. There is no change in my true state of being.

There is only change in outpictured imaginal experience.

I am not thoughts.

I am not images I see in my imagination.

I am not sensory impressions.

I am not memories.

I am not experiences.

I am not what I do.

I am not how I behave.

I am not subject to others behavior or false rules.

I am not subjugated, nor may I be contained, constrained, limited, or bounded.

I am part and parcel of the one-mind. I live and dwell in oneness. I grasp with my entire attention the connection I feel to the one-mind and all living power.

The one-mind is eternal. Therefore, who I am in truth is eternal.

I am not the instrument I call my physical body. I identify with the power of my being, the beginning of life, and the origin of all worlds.

I see my place in oneness. I see my purpose in oneness. I see all events, experiences, and conditions in their true place in oneness.

Distressed - Collected

I am collected. Every aspect of my mind is in the presence of oneness. All aspects of my life are resolved and complete and whole. I am whole in the entirety of my being. I am part and parcel of the one-mind. From the beginning, I am recognized, treasured, and important.

All my affairs are settled in one-mind. All activities are perfectly directed. All my good is designated and appointed for me in one-mind.

I am known in one-mind and endowed with the faculties of mind to think in alignment with truth.

I think with understanding. I use decision making capacity with full awareness of understanding. I am intelligent creative awareness and use my imaginative faculty to design an experience that feels resolved, informed, and centered.

I pause and focus my attention. I breathe steadily. I quiet my mind by calming the flow of mental activity. I focus my attention on the power of my being, the infinite, expansive, inherent intelligence that can see, hear, and feel into the true reality of the one-mind.

In this state of being, there is no worry; there is no hurry. There is only silence, stillness, and oneness. There is everlasting peace, unconditioned awareness, and unity.

In this state of being, I feel at ease. I feel circulating, radiating power. I digest truth and assimilate the perfect pattern of wisdom into my body-mind.

Disturbed - Aligned

I am aligned with the one-mind through my eternal connection. I am never lost. I am never alone. I am surrounded and embodied with the radiating power of my being.

I am aligned with the eternal source of intelligent thought. I can only see, hear, and feel intelligent thoughts. I am personally known in one-mind. I am comforted and my attention is guided to dwell on only that which is good.

I go forth into new realms of experience. I am aligned with my good. I enter into a new world of intelligent self-awareness and all is well.

I dwell in a fortress of serenity. I am placid and stable minded. My thoughts reflect truth and I speak only eternal truths.

I recognize myself and all parties for who they are: distinct self-aware parts of the one-mind.

I allow all illusions of disconnection, separation, ignorance, and selfishness to dissolve in the light of the truth that we are all one.

I am aligned with what is right for me.

I nurture my connection with the origin of all wisdom. I am aware of my connection with the origin of truth.

I release all false conceptions and they immediately fall lifeless in my trail.

Ahead of me is my everlasting, unending potential.

I turn my attention to the good that is available to me. I allow it to enter into the temple of my inner world where I give my good life, form, and substance. I use my power only to express good. I use my power only to entertain truthful thoughts. I use the instrument I call my physical body to express desirable moods and feelings. I train my physical body to act on only that which is good.

I have forgotten all false concepts of myself, origin, life, and all parties. I seek only the good in myself and in all. The act of love is the mindful application of truth in my experience.

I no longer deceive myself and thereby no longer attempt to deceive others. It is impossible for me to speak falsely. It is impossible for me to act upon false thoughts. Every aspect of my mind is aligned with the origin of all truth.

Through the power inherent in me, I give truth means of expression and experience good experiences one after another.

I recall all past experiences with wisdom, understanding, and clarity. I forgive myself and all for acting in states of undesirable moods.

All is well.

Dizzy - Stabled

My mind is centered and stable.

I am firmly planted upon the foundation of truth which is the power of my being.

I sit and sense the power of my being and I feel the flow of everlasting life moving through me.

My attention is centered on stabled thoughts that stabilize the conditions of my experiences.

The conditions of my life reflect stability. The conditions of my life reflect steady growth and greater evolution to the full understanding of oneness.

I am full of unending, steady power. I emanate power into every interaction with all parties.

I feel free from external influence. I feel free of all affectation.

There is no external person, force, mind, or obstruction that can separate me from the presence of the one-mind. I live and dwell peacefully in the presence of my being knowing that it forever is connected to the one-mind.

My breathing is steady and stable. The flow of my blood and other fluids is steady and stable. The movement of my body-mind is easy and patterned after the serenity of the one-mind.

I feel suspended in the power of my being. I feel supported, safe, and embraced by oneness.

My mind thinks slowly and deliberately upon thoughts of unity and oneness.

I am engaged with those in my experience in a harmonious way. I hold within the center of my being endless appreciation for the power of my being as it flows ever more into my experience.

Doubt - Expect

The whole world works together to help me achieve my goals. I hear happy news. I always get what I choose. Everyone, especially me, knows that something good is on my way and guaranteed to be delivered at a specified moment.

Everything is working out in perfect order and in perfect timing to meet me where I am directed to be.

Everyone in the world gets exactly what they align their mental arrangements with in the most efficient way.

I am heard and immediately answered. The animating substance of all forms always responds to and forms itself according to my words.

Tasks are complete in perfect order and timing. Means and ways are provided for and illuminated for all involved.

The power of my being is at ease, invigorating, and calm. I am free to experience other things while instructions are being fulfilled.

I let go of all concern and mental preoccupation in favor of peace of mind.

Doubtful - Wield

I wield the power that I am. I am loyal to the power that I am. I trust the power in me to fulfill my commands. I accept completely that I am connected to and a part of the origin of all. My faith shows me that I remember this fundamental truth.

I feel the power in me, that is me. I wield it wisely. I am aware of the power of my being.

Wielding the power of my being gives expression to those assumptions that I hold as the operative commands directing the movement of my mind. I journey to those realms where my attention goes. I do what I first do in imagination.

I have complete faith in my existence as a life giving force. I do not doubt that I create as I command with my directed imagination. My words affirm that which I determine is to be. I shape my reality with my words. My words form my experience. I wield my word accurately.

I decide my next experience. I create what and the moment I decide. My decisions are actions. My decisions animate the power of my being. I am the force that gives form motion. I am power and presence. I naturally create and bring into my experience that which I conceive is beautiful and loving.

I move the unseen into the seen. Reality conforms to the arrangement of my mind. I take form after my own self-conceptions, but I know that I am not these forms. I am what gives form.

I am calm, still, and serene in this awareness of my true nature. I am the indwelling presence of the origin of awareness. As this power embodied, I can do all. I see as this power. In wielding the power that I am, I express my nature. I experience everything as this power.

Drained - Sustained

The empowering presence of my being sustains the instrument I call my physical body. I feel a strong, steady current of power flowing from the origin of power through my distinct mind and into my world. This power completes me. This power fills my body and animates it.

I am sustained and therefore I sustain all endeavors that express my good. My growth in understanding is sustained by the eternal power available to me. My mind is continually renewed. My physical body is continually renewed.

My imagination is renewed with refreshing clarity. My perception and recollection of experiences is pure and based upon truth. I maintain thoughts that sustain me. My mind focuses on dreams that sustain goodness in my experience.

Sustaining vitality pervades all areas of my world.

My relationships are sustained by truthful interactions and a shared feeling of unity. The unity of the one-mind connects us all and sustains our connection as distinct self-aware parts of the one mind.

I can never be cut off from one-mind or from others entirely. I am sustained by our shared connection and can access that at any time. Therefore, I am always connected to the origin of all knowing and can obtain knowledge from the origin at any time.

Drunk - Sympathy

My mind is clear.

I am free from all false and deceptive thinking.

I am free from the habit of thinking destructive thoughts. I free myself from corrosive attitudes and behaviors.

I orient my attention on beautiful thoughts of myself and all parties. I direct my attention to create lovely mental scenes and imaginal designs. I command my imagination to construct scenes of harmony, elegance, and ease.

I relate to others with sympathy. I recognize the unity of all parties. I feel and recognize the connection we all share in one-mind.

I use my attention and engage my imagination to envision positive interactions with all. I feel well in my being, settled, center, calm, and serene. I am centered in the present. I am oriented towards truth.

I relax my mind and slow down my mental actions. I breathe softly. I open up all pathways in my mind and discharge myself of all obstructions and obstacles that create mental limitations.

I make experiences easy for myself. I simplify my experiences.

I am simplicity experiencing myself.

I am serenity experiencing myself.

I am transformative power experiencing myself.

I am who I am. I am who I want to be. I love who I am. I love what I create.

I love all parties as myself because we are all one in one-mind.

I set my attention free to experience new lovely experiences. I release the past and all deceptive memories that would have me believe that I am something that I am not.

I am not the thoughts that I think.

I am not the experiences I experienced.

I am oneness incarnate; self-aware creative intelligence and I decide to experience myself in only beautiful forms.

I love myself and give to myself all that is good.

I feel the power of love in me that can dissolve all false thinking.

I clear my mind and rest my mind. Good is at work in my world.

Everything I need is within me.

I access the depths of my being and feel that which I decide to experience.

Dysentery - Digest

I digest the truth into experience and I reject all wasteful thinking.

Wasteful thinking is all thinking that squanders my power into creating deceptive thoughtforms.

I automatically and immediately disintegrate all false thoughtforms from my mind.

I release myself from the effects of deceptive thinking. My entire mind is aligned with pure thoughts and the source of pure thoughts which is the origin of all perfect patterns.

I use my power to create in my inner world imaginal designs that are beautiful, pleasing, and affirming of the truth of my nature.

I do not accept into my inner world false thinking.

I do not turn my attention away from the one-mind. I do not cast myself off by turning my attention away from the one mind and creating false thoughtforms in my imagination.

I do not allow false thoughts believed by other parties to enter into my mind and perpetuate into my experience.

I cast away all false thoughts and acceptance of false conditions. I release the belief that an external power has control over me.

I destroy all false conditions. I destroy all false thought forms. My body-mind is pure and I create purity through the application of the power of my being in my experience. I release from the arrangement of my mind any thoughts that would have me turn my attention away from my good. I focus attentively on my good and dwell upon beautiful thoughts to create a mood of serenity, harmony, and relaxation.

I allow the power of my being to amplify the beauty I construct in my imagination. I am centered, stabled, and rooted firmly in the feeling of oneness.

Dysfunction - Organization

My attention is perfectly fixed upon the feeling of organization in every experience.

Perfect patterns are available for me to attune the power of my being and give form into my experience. I am intently aligned with the organization of all good expressed in oneness.

I feel with my inner senses the perfect organization of all completed concepts.

I recognize and understand with clarity of thought all perfect patterns.

I can express all perfect patterns. I understand the organization of all forms. I decipher all scrambled forms. I clarify all obscured conditions.

I am perfectly organized. My mind is perfectly organized.

My dwelling is perfectly organized. Every aspect of my experience is perfectly organized.

I function harmoniously. My body-mind is organized. My activities are organized. Each perfect thought that I accept generates perfect forms.

Because I am organized, each action I take benefits the next. I am ever increasing in ease and functionality. I perform greater and greater acts with greater and greater ease. I am able to accomplish more complex tasks because my mind is perfectly organized with wisdom.

I recognize how everything in my experience is organized. I recognize how everything in my experience is created and expressed.

I have perfect understanding at all times. I am forever aligned with the truth of my nature.

I employ the power of my being to express truth in my experience.

I bring order to the illusion of chaos.

I dispel all deceptive moods.

E
Earned - Granted

My good is apportioned for me out of the eternal, infinite, and everlasting bounty of the one-mind.

Everything good and enters into my experience was first designated in one-mind. Everything that enters into my outer world of experience enters into my imagination from the origin of all perfect forms.

A thought form enters into my awareness. The form's pattern is felt and accepted by me. And, it then is materialized by the amplification of the perfect pattern by the power of my being.

Like an egg fertilized by a spermatozoa, the power of my being moves to give form and dimension to the arrangement of my mind by which the light that shines from me may show me what I have created in my own individual experience.

Without my acceptance, nothing enters into my experience.

Without my permission, no condition or form rests in my experience. I give form and expression to thoughtforms that are pleasing to me.

With my attention, I direct the power of my being to those thoughtforms that are patterned after the likeness of truth. Every materialized form that enters into my awareness was granted entrance into my experience by me.

I receive my good with an open mind. I am open to new experiences that usher in my good.

I am worthy of receiving all that is beautiful, perfect, and exceptional.

I easily and simply experience my good now in my imagination.

With my inner feeling, I sense the pattern of the form that I will generate. I sense it with my inner awareness. I can see, hear, feel, and touch using my inner senses and thus create imaginal experiences that affirm the fulfillment of my good in my inner world.

There is no external force or mind that can prevent the fulfillment of my good from coming into my experience. I claim my good and affirm its reality in my innerworld and know when my good is prepared to enter into my experience.

There is no surprise as to when my good will be fully expressed. I feel its gestation in the womb of my inner world. I automatically and intuitively feel the connection with my good, like a mother and her unborn baby. I know when my good will come into my experience and when it is ready.

I am always ready to receive my good. I prepare for its reception with patience, poise, and serenity.

I feel connected to all good that is immediately available to me.

Enemy - Self

There is no enemy.

There is only the self.

There exists only the concept of my capacities in relation to my concept of others' capacities.

By the application of self through the imaginal activities, we are all capable of creating experiences of all kinds.

All are one because we all are composed of and connected to the only power in existence.

There is no other. There is no separate power. There is no external mind.

There is only the capacity of creative expression by which I accept thoughts and instruct my actions.

All self-aware parts of the one-mind possess this faculty of expression. There is no otherness, only variation of expression.

Manners of expression reveal my chosen mood.

I am not my mood, nor I am not the thoughts or feelings I experience. all self-aware distinct parts of the one-mind are witnesses to my expression.

I see myself for who I am. I see all parties for who they are and how we all belong together.

I release all false conceptions of separation, division, and externality.

There is only unity. There is only wholeness.

I am one. All are one. All is one.

Error - Correct

Correct use of my imagination always guarantees desired results. I only activate my imagination to create good in my experience. I only activate the power of my being in receptivity to the good available to me.

All thoughts from the origin of joy, vitality, and prosperity steadily and infinitely stream into my attention. My decision to experience joy, vitality, and prosperity seals the instructions for their fulfillment into my experience. My decision to experience joy, vitality, and prosperity creates a perfect pattern transmitted through the instrument I call my physical body into the realm of form. I give form to perfect ideas.

I see perfect images. I hear perfect sounds. I feel perfect sensations. I give all of these expressions in the realm of outer experience.

When I say the word "correct", my attention immediately aligns every part of my being with the origin of perfection.

My physical body operates correctly. My mind operates correctly.

The correct process of creation is the manner in which my attention becomes more and more aligned with the completion state of all good.

All good already exists within the one-mind. My only task is to concentrate my attention on that which already exists in perfection and completion.

Through this activity, the power of my being amplifies perfect patterns and transmits them through the instrument I call my physical body into the realm of outer experience. This correct process is also called prayer; activating my receptivity to good and connecting to it in oneness.

Correct use of my attention blots out all misshapen thought forms. Correct use of my physical body eliminates all sickness. Correct use of moods creates an infinite number of good experiences.

All is one with good. I experience it as so.

Excuses - Solutions

I am aligned with the origin of all solutions.

Solutions come through my connection with the origin of all ideas and into my experience through which I may employ the instrument of my physical body to bring into shared experience new thought and action.

Solutions are merely new thoughts introduced to act in an inventive way. I am inventive because I am open to new means of expression. I am inventive because I am open to new manners of behavior.

I delight myself with new actions that reflect my natural capacities. Each day is new, fresh, and shows me how the arrangement of my mind is evolving into steadfast conscious awareness of my connection with the origin of being.

Everyday is new because I renew my mind daily. I approach each imaginative design with a clear mind that is receptive to innovative ideas.

I hold fast to my connection with the origin of creation and create in accordance to concepts that increase a shared awareness of and connection to each other in oneness with the whole.

I bring to my attention my intended goals and maintain their completion in my mind.

I allow my connection to the power of invention to present to me clear plans for the fulfillment of my goals. Upon seeing these plans I venture with new thought and action for the fulfillment of my goals. Each step is clearly presented and understood and I know intuitively and immediately what to do to fulfill its execution.

I endeavor nothing else except the fulfillment of my good. I receive no other thoughts except inspiration that form the means by which to accomplish my goals. I hear no other voice except that of the origin of thought to guide my decisions and influence my actions. I am one with the origin of solutions and thus I am the solution to any opportunity for expanded understanding.

Solutions enter into my experience every day. Solutions contain their instructions for the fulfillment. Solutions are simple to implement and enjoyable to fulfill. Solutions always find me and approach me all the time.

I recognize solutions instantly and immediately put them into implementation in my experience. I am recognized for my solution oriented nature. I encourage others to recognize and implement solutions in their own experience.

All solutions are contained in the inner consciousness of my being. I go into my inner consciousness and am rewarded openly when I allow them to come through the instrument of my body.

I receive solution-based thoughts. I speak solutions. I act out solutions. I see solutions realized each new day.

Solutions are already formed and I increase my attention to solutions with each moment.

Exasperated - Ease

I am free to express my true self.

I move naturally. I breathe easily.

I behave according to my true nature.

I carry myself with ease of mind. My mind is still.

With joy of being, I relax and enjoy every experience into which I enter.

My imagination is full of harmonious, perfectly organized designs intending to aid me in the fullest expression of my true nature.

Each experience brings to me a greater sense of serenity. I feel an ever increasing focus on all that is my good. I feel an ever increasing strength of understanding to my connection to all.

I feel the goodness in all. I recognize the beauty in all. I feel the power that connects us all.

Each new experience brings to me an ever greater understanding of joy, beauty, harmony, and camaraderie with all.

I enjoy every interaction in my world. I have fun in every experience.

I fill each experience with my presence, animating interactions with pleasantness.

Exhausted - Restored

The power of my being strips away and dissolves all false conditions impressed upon my mind and therefore evaporates all false and deceptive conditions.

All false conditions of mind exit my experience.

All relationships based upon false assumptions are immediately restored to truth.

All false thoughtforms disappear in my inner world which immediately results in the disappearance of all false thoughtforms from my outer world.

I call forth the power of truth, of oneness, of presence - which are all one - to restore my mind to its perfect state.

The total arrangement of mind is in agreement, congruence, and alignment with the perfect state of being.

I am aware of my true nature. I am aware of my true essence. I am aware of my true expression.

My entire body-mind exists in enduring peace and rests in this state of permanent wholeness.

I maintain my attention on the origin of oneness.

My understanding of oneness is ever increasing. Thus, my experience of oneness is ever increasing.

There is no conflict in my mind. There is no conflict in the total arrangement of my mind. There is no conflict or argument in the arrangement of my mind.

Every distinct part of the instrument I call my physical body is in cooperation with truth everlastingly and perpetually.

I am wholly focused on the truth of oneness.

Expel - Integrate

I am an indispensable, integral, important part of the whole.

I am part and parcel with the one-mind. I am a distinct, self-aware part of one-mind.

I recognize my place in oneness. I feel oneness in my entire experience.

I feel fulfilled in the truth of my being.

There is no division in one mind. There is no exclusion in one-mind. I am accepted in one-mind. I am valuable, important, distinguished, and an integral part of the fulfillment of oneness in all experience.

I am whole in all forms. I am complete in all forms.

I participate in the fulfillment of my true nature in my outer world. I feel a sense of togetherness and participation in all experiences.

I feel included, valued, and recognized for the goodness I exude from the presence of my being.

I can never be excluded. I can never be rejected.

I accept who I am and my nature of being. I accept all that is my good for it is all contained within the power of my being. I feel my connection with all parties in one-mind. I feel the true essence of my being and sense the eternal appreciation of expression in all forms.

I turn my attention away from all false constructions of thought based in the rejection of truth. I release my attention from all illusory thoughtforms and redirect my participation in the fulfillment of good in my world.

I feel included in the accomplishment of good and the realization of ever higher vistas of understanding.

Exploit - Empower

I know who I truly am.

I understand my nature, my capacities, and my capabilities.

I understand my own worth. I recognize my endowment. I recognize my inherent mental faculties of which I am empowered to use.

I know what I am capable of doing. I know how to use my imagination to form imaginal designs based upon thoughts aligned with the origin of all truth.

I know how to use my sensing faculties to feel for perfect forms in my inner world and bring them into experience in my outer world.

I revoke all permission to participate in deceptive unions. I remove the presence of my being from all relationships based upon illusions.

I disintegrate false conditions. All false conditions disintegrate in the light of the truth to which I am permanently aligned.

I remember that I am formless, shapeless awareness - a life giving force - that is part and parcel with the one-mind.

I am known, honored, esteemed, and valued in one-mind. I am endowed with the creative powers of the one-mind to fulfill my good and to create for myself the experience of my choosing.

I am the master of my own experience. I determine what thoughts enter into my inner world.

I release from my awareness all deceptive thoughts and illusions. I only see the truth of oneness in my experience. I can only feel for and experience perfect thoughts.

I free my attention from all mental captivity. I free my attention from all limiting thoughts. I free my attention and the power of my being from all false feelings.

All is well. All is one.

I am part and parcel of the whole. The power of my being is complete, perfect and good.

The arrangement of my mind is attuned with the one-mind and expresses the character of the oneness.

F
Fatigue - Radiant

I am radiant because I am light. The power of my being radiates through the instrument I call my physical body.

My presence is light.

The one-mind contains all of creation which is complete, accomplished, and in a state of perfection.

My distinct mental arrangement reflects the qualities of the one-mind.

Through my inherent endowment of mental faculties and my ceaseless connection to the one-mind in which all are one, I feel the everlasting pulsation of animating power that is available to me.

I direct the power of my being in the fullest expression of my true nature.

I engage in the activities that create perfect experiences.

The presence of my being dissolves all false conditions. The direction in which I orient the power of my being brings perfection, truth, and understanding.

I radiate the true essence of my being. I speak truth. I act in truth.

Under perfect instruction, I complete my good. I experience in my inner world beautiful constructions that express themselves through the power of my being and into my outer world.

I feel energized, empowered, and directed to move my physical body in perfect harmony and poise.

I feel good in my being. I feel good in my body. My physical body reflects the goodness upon which my attention dwells. I feel with my inner senses stillness, calm, and circulating joy of being.

I am enthusiastic in my ways. I am confident in my ways.

I am one with all. I feel my oneness with all.

I feel my oneness with the one-mind that is the origin and eternal source of vitality, renewal, and reinvigoration.

Fatigued - Energized

I am self-aware power of being.

The instrument I call my physical body is energized. The revitalizing energy from the origin of all intelligent power flows through me. I feel the goodness of my being. I feel vital because I am vitality incarnate.

The joy of my being shines into my world. I smile with my entire mind.

I am energized by unending power. I wake up refreshed and directed to fulfill my good. I am capable of any endeavor I decide to fulfill. I feel intelligent power directing my physical body in the fulfillment of my good.

I am propelled in positive action. I move in harmony with my good. My physical body is healthy, vibrant, and communicative of the truth of my being.

My thoughts are wholesome, loving, and joyful.

My body-mind is an instrument for the transmission of joy, serenity, and wisdom. I *feel* the qualities of joy, serenity, and wisdom. The qualities of these moods are the unique patterns of expression of the origin of creative expression. Good moods are expressions of creative intelligent energy like a kaleidoscope of color and light.

Everyday, my mind and physical body are renewed. I maintain a steady stream of vitality, strength, poise, and correct movement. I cannot fail. I succeed in the fulfillment of my good as an expression of unrestricted energy.

My energy flows through my individual experience and into my outer world giving shape and form to my good. Every organ of my physical body is in harmony with this intelligent power that is I am.

I produce the image and likeness of perfect organization and vitality.

All is well in mind and all is well in my physical body, the extension of my mind.

Fear - Serene

There is no external mind. There is no external power. There is no other.

There is no otherness. There is no division. There is no power save for the power and presence of the one-mind.

I release the total arrangement of my mind from the repression, deception, disease, and all reflections of thought born out of false assumptions and rejection of my true nature.

I am made in the reflection of the origin of creative, intelligent presence.

I feel the powerful presence of the one-mind living and breathing as me. I live and dwell in the light of the origin of light. I live and dwell in the origin of all truth.

I shall never again be swayed by false thoughts. I shall never be held captive by deceptive thinking.

I orient my attention to the presence of the one-mind. I feel the goodness, personal knowing, and gentleness of the one-mind expressed through me and through all.

All experiences reveal to me the origin of the thought pattern from which it came.

I select beautiful experiences and experience them with all my sensory faculties. In the temple of my inner world I feel stillness, calm, serenity, and perfect completion.

All is well. All is finished.

I erase all false feelings associated with past experiences. I re-imagine all undesirable memories with perfect completion.

I decide what experiences are acceptable to me. I create perfect experiences in my imagination. I touch from within the depths of the perfect stillness within me all that is excellent, magnificent, and superfluent.

I cast away all doubtful thinking and turn my attention to the expectation of the fulfillment of my good. The power of my being obeys my command. Thus, I use my word to affirm the direction of my attention.

I refuse external authorities. I refuse to accept defeat. I accept only serenity for I am serene.

Fed Up - Ready

I now enter into the next phase of my life. My mind is already there, my experience is now transforming to reflect this next area of awareness. I have finished with the past, the old, and outmoded. I am always entering where my attention has first gone in presence and it is always good.

I no longer feel the old ways of feeling. I no longer think the old ways of thinking.

My mind receives new ideas that rejuvenate how I experience myself and all. I see and know my circumstances are improving. I notice with acuity how events work out for me and I now fully understand this fact.

I am ready and complete. There is nothing more for me to do than remember that I have my good now.

The origin of all good already created my good. The origin of all good simply rests until I allow my good to enter into my experience through my imagination. It is with expectancy that I receive my good now. I do not have to wait, I have my good now in its richness and fullness of expression.

I have everything I need now. I have what it takes to fulfill my good now. I am ready, qualified, and able at every phase of experience. I am and will always be ready for that which is my good. I am emotionally ready, mature, and capable of experiencing my good. I have what it takes because I was born with what it takes to imagine my good.

If I can imagine my good, I can experience it.

Fixate - Release

I release all false thought forms that express suffering.

I release all false assumptions that distract me from the truth of my nature.

I release my attention from all false constructions of thought.

I disengage the power of my being from all organizations based upon deception.

I release all thoughts inconsistent with perfect peace, serenity, movement.

I reorient my attention to all the capacities endowed in me by the very nature of my being as part and parcel to the infinite intelligent creative presence of oneness.

I release my attention from old patterns of thinking. I release the entirety of the arrangement of my mind from all false premises that would have me act in a manner inconsistent with my true nature as intelligent, creative power of being.

All distorted memories fade away in the light of truth. I realize my attention from disorienting attitudes of mind. I am affixed to the stability and firmness of oneness.

I am centered. I am constituted of perfection.

I take pleasure in the fullness of expressing my nature which is intelligence, creativity, beauty, wholeness, gentleness, and grace.

Force - Gravitate

I am aware of all the good that is available in the power of my presence.

I can feel all manner of forms within the one-mind. I can touch with my inner sensing faculties all that is good and know that I may experience it in my outer world of form.

There is no experience, no creative form that exists outside of me. I feel goodness within me at all times.

I always intently focus my attention and thus direct my power of being in the expression of all good.

My movements are directed by intelligence. My words are formed to be the perfect reflection of wisdom. My choices are aligned with the one-mind to express oneness in all its forms.

All that is good, beautiful, lovely, and perfect is available to me to enjoy.

All that is fun, pleasurable, expansive, and fine is available to me to experience.

I release all barriers of attention that would obscure my vision and dull my sensing faculties.

I release all conceptions of division so that I may enter into the experience of oneness with all that is my good.

Forget - Recall

I have a perfect recall.

I access in my imagination images, sounds, words, thoughts, and events at command. When I instruct my imagination to show me something, my imagination immediately responds with the corresponding answer.

My mind never fails me. My memory never fails me. My imagination never fails me.

My mind always answers. My memory is always revealed. My imagination always answers.

The origin of all imagery, thought, sound, and conceptual understanding always meets my attention and provides forms for me to use for my fulfillment.

I recall details easily. I recall information easily and use it to construct new experiences. I recall experiences and get new insight to enhance new experiences. I live in the eternal present and thus all knowledge is available to me.

I know the correct questions to ask to get the answers I desire to recall. I recall information from the origin of all information.

I understand the information I recall naturally. I recall naturally and release all holds on my attention so that I may recall instantly, naturally, and with vivid clarity.

I see in my imagination answers to questions. I recognize perfectly expressed forms in my imagination.

I imagine what I desire to experience and the power of my being recalls information to construct a scene which would indicate the fulfillment of that experience. As I recall with great detail, the scene becomes integrated into my mental arrangement as an event that I create with the power of my being. I recall all details and experience them as events unfolding from my imagination.

I recall the creative forces of nature to come together to supply that which I command to create.

My experiences are a coming together of the creative forces that fulfill my decisions. With immediacy, accuracy, and perfect organization my decisions become my reality. I have a perfect understanding of this process. I remember the decisions that create my experiences. I decide to recall those experiences that are good for me and others. Thus, I recall all goodness.

Fret - Focused

I am focused entirely on the truth that is inherent and expressed in oneness.

I integrate the truth expressed by the one-mind into my own distinct self-awareness and allow all truth to impress upon the arrangement of my mind all patterns of expression amplified by the instrument I call my physical body.

My physical body is the instrument through which the patterns of perfection are made manifest in my outer world. I focus my attention on perfect patterns. I see perfect patterns in total completion in original wholeness.

I magnify and glorify greater truths one after another and experience them first in my inner world.

I feel the goodness, light, and joy that emanates between my inner experience to my outer world.

I correct all distorted thoughts, false assumptions, and misunderstanding with neutralizing truth.

I feel activated, motivated, and empowered by the power of my being. My attention focused on these inner sensations increases in my experience and I immediately observe my outer world conforming to these organizing patterns.

The total arrangement of my mind is organized to amplify perfect patterns into my experience. I gain ever greater vistas of understanding, wisdom, and mastery.

My habits of thought are directed by instructions to fulfill solely on expressions of oneness. The nature of oneness is an expression of my true character as part and parcel of the one-mind.

My true nature is at ease with all for there is only oneness of being. All illusion of separation is a false projection of a mind refusing to accept their true nature of oneness.

I am focused entirely on expressing my true nature. I am focused entirely on the power of my being. I think according to my true nature. I behave in accordance with my true nature.

I fulfill the instructions of my true nature.

I enjoy good living in accordance with my true nature.

I reflect the true reality of oneness.

Frightened - Assured

My attention is directly focused upon the truth of oneness. I can feel oneness through the presence of my being.

I focus my attention intently on my inner feelings of calmness, steadiness, and centeredness.

I gather thoughts of good and accept them into the temple of my inner being.

I build upon feelings of serenity, developing in my imagination scenes indicating the fulfillment of my good.

I am assured that I am heard in one-mind.

I am known, recognized, esteemed, and valued in one-mind.

Thoughts of good that I recognize, accept, and speak in the womb of my inner world develop into patterns that emanate through the instrument I call my physical body.

I can feel the patterns of good thoughts that come directly from the one-mind, the origin of all truth, shifting and rearranging the arrangement of my mind and bringing about the fulfillment of that good into my outer world.

I reject all false thoughts from my mind. I reject the presence of all false conditions. I deny all false authority. All deceptive thoughtforms crumble in my presence and at my command.

The light of my presence shines upon all deception which fades all shadows of doubt, worry, and fear.

All is well. All is one.

Frustration - Progress

I progress in all ways at all times.

My power of my being goes forth and advances my cause. My imaginal designs are developing in clarity every day. My imaginal designs are developing in expression in my world.

I progress in all realms of fulfillment. I am progressive.

New information, ideas, and concepts come to my attention in progression, helping me to build new imaginal designs that reflect my ever increasing conception of my true nature.

Greater and greater concepts capture my attention and enter into the temple of my inner being to be expressed through me and in my outer world.

Greater concepts of beauty, truth, and goodness never cease to capture my attention. My actions are based upon greater concepts of truth.

I advance in fulfillment at every moment. I progress ceaselessly, effortlessly, and peacefully. I see the development of my good in every experience. The conditions of my world further my understanding and my mind grows in truth and in light.

In ever increasing ways, I progress. My world arranges itself to reveal my self concept to me.

I achieve the fulfillment of my decisions at all times. I see myself progressing. I see my endeavors progressing.

I sense my connection to the one-mind and all therein. I am satisfied at every stage of progression. I see my wholeness at every stage of progression.

I trust my capacity to progress. I trust my inherent power to evolve in self-understanding.

Furious - Dynamic

The power of my being is a dynamic presence not limited by thoughts of temporary conditions.

What comes next is not determined by present conditions or circumstances.

I decide what comes next by deciding what to accept now as my reality.

I place no external power authority over me, my actions, my decisions, and my potential.

I withdraw all permission from all conditions upon which I have attached my state of being.

I sever the total arrangement of my mind from all dependencies and conditional attachments.

I turn my attention away from false assumptions in separate powers, external minds, and illusions of control.

I recreate the arrangement of my mind and recreate my world.

I renew the arrangement of my mind by turning my attention to all that is true, all that is permanent, and all that is integritous.

I have all that I need within the power of my being. I turn my attention to the power of my being and witness the grandeur, delight, beauty, and intelligence emanating from the presence of my being.

I feel the oneness of all. I feel the truth contained therein.

I am free to move my attention in any direction. I am free to expand past present modes of thinking. I am free to explore the depths of oneness beyond the present arrangement of my mind.

I receive new ideas that transform the arrangement of my mind.

I experience even greater experiences of oneness.

G
Grief - Enveloped

I feel the embrace of the one-mind.

I feel the infinite present loving attention from my sense of oneness with all.

There is no separation from that which I feel appreciation, gratitude, and inclusion.

There is only one. All are one.

I am connected to all through my connection shared in one-mind.

Illusions of separation and division depart from me. False thoughtforms representing loss, disruption, and despair dissolve in the light of my being.

With clarity, I perceive and recognize the intimate connection I share in one-mind with all.

Thoughts of shared joy, shared experiences, and shared connection flood my imagination bringing to me wonderful memories and lasting feelings of fulfillment.

I sense the vastness of appreciation and the inescapable presence of all who I love emanating their shared appreciation of me. Through my personal experience of oneness I feel the intelligent presence of the one-mind. I am known in one-mind. We are never separated, divided, or parted. We are always one.

Grip - Space

I fill my world with my presence.

I am large, grand, and embodied in the power of my being.

The power of my being goes before me and expands into all my world.

The power of my being is not limited by the form and shape of the instrument I call my physical body.

The light of my being illuminates my outer world.

The one-mind pervades and inhabits all distinct minds to fulfill itself in the dream we all share as one.

I fill every space I enter into. I animate every experience.

My presence reverberates through the instrument I call my physical body and emanates the pattern of the assumptions I accept as true.

I clarify all false conditions. I stabilize all false patterns. I loosen all gripping false thoughtforms. I release the hold of my attention from all that is inconsistent with truth.

Grudge - Mercy

I bring understanding, ease, and grace to every condition and to every interaction.

When I witness a false condition or encounter a party under the illusion of false thinking, I emanate truthful thoughts that reorient all distinct self-aware minds towards the origin of truth. I feel the presence of the origin of all life. I hear the voice of the one-mind directing me with truthful instructions. I resolve any conflict. I bring serenity, peace, and harmony to any conflict.

Forgiveness is a natural byproduct of turning my attention away from false thoughts. I feel the renewing, revitalizing, cleansing feeling of oneness restoring the arrangement of my mind to a state of clarity. I feel cleared of all deceptive thoughts. I have lifted myself up from deceptive thinking and dissolved all barriers to my attention.

I feel present and centered in this moment. I feel mentally quiet and oriented. I feel stable and settled in the power of my being. I feel the perfect pattern of truth circulating throughout my entire body-mind. I feel my body-mind aligning with the origin of all organized thought and I function in perfect cooperation with the one-mind.

I use my mind correctly. I use the instrument I call my physical body correctly. I listen to only truthful thoughts. I feel for and sense only truthful forms. I am in touch with an eternally loving oneness from which I will never separate from again. I feel my oneness with all parties. I feel my oneness with the one-mind.

I correct deceptive thinking by using my inner senses to feel liberating forms. I feel liberated from the inside out.

My mind is liberated and goes anywhere in time, space, and dimension. I am unlimited, boundaryless, and boundless.

All is well. All are one.

H
Hallucination - Awake

I am perfectly awake. I am perfectly aware of my true nature. I am aware of the ever unfolding understanding of what is available in me to experience.

I turn my attention away from all that is false, deceptive, and unreal.

I release the power of my being from all false patterns and false constructions of thought that would have my attention distracted from the fulfillment of my true nature in the outer world of experience.

I see clearly. I hear perfectly. I feel the purest sensations emanating from the power of my being which is part and parcel with the oneness of all.

Through an intentional connection with the one-mind I perceive my good at all times. I decipher all communications that I sense from within me. I discern all that I experience in the outer world of experience with clarity and excellent judgment.

I wisely articulate that which I am aware of being. I am able to turn my attention to focus upon that which I deem is acceptable and preferable to me.

There is no external power that has authority over my experiences and sensations. There is no other mind determining and deciding for me that which I shall experience.

I revoke all permission from those concepts to which I have surrendered my decision making faculty. I revoke all permission from all parties that I have given permission to decide where I direct my attention. No one has control or authority over where I direct my attention.

I reclaim my mental faculties. I reclaim the use and direction over the power of my being.

My mind is perfectly organized. The instrument I call my physical body is a perfect reflection of the harmonious organization of my mental arrangement.

I release all false assumptions from the total arrangement of my mind that are in direct conflict with the perfection of the one-mind. My body-mind functions to reveal the vast and infinite bounty available in oneness.

I feel my oneness with all. I feel my personal and intimate connection with the one-mind.

There is no other reality except oneness. I live and dwell in oneness and in perfect harmony with all.

Hard - Moveable

My attention is moveable and flexible. I can move my attention to any destination, event, and space of experience. I direct my attention to any result I deem worthy of experience.

I freely and easily move my attention to the origin of all thought. I can move my mind in any direction. I see in all directions. I see into any form and thus know what I desire to know.

I see the arrangement of my mind clearly. I rearrange the structure of my mind into a pleasing pattern. The pattern forms my expression. My self-conception reveals to me the mechanism that directs my power to build experiences according to my assumptions.

I command my attention to see what I instruct it to see. I can organize my mind to fulfill my imaginative designs with the use of my words.

I organize words to construct my world. With every word I think and thus speak with my mind I become aware of even greater parts of a new world that I have created for myself to dwell in.

I move my attention away from all obstacles, blockages, and limitations. I instruct my attention and thus my body-mind to move. I move gracefully, easily, and smoothly. I move instantaneously and thus begin a chain of events that unfold the fulfillment of my good.

I move towards greater feelings of freedom. I expand the territory of my mind and thus the arrangement of my mind to greater realms of knowledge. I move my attention beyond all limitations. I dissolve all limitations when I move my attention.

Harm - Restore

I restore all images to their intended, perfect form as designed in oneness.

I turn my attention to perfect images and recognize the perfection inherent and endowed in all parties.

I restore my mind to perfect functioning by orienting my attention to the oneness that restores all from the deception of false images, constructions, and ideas.

I sense the essence of my true nature. I see my true self in my imagination.

I can perceive with my mind's eye the perfect functioning of the instrument that I call my physical body.

I correct all undesirable memories with new, beautiful images of pleasant interactions.

I see with my mind's eye the wholeness, goodness, and elegance of every aspect of my world.

I transform every false thought and feeling with the power of my being. I release all false restraints of mind. I release all thoughts inconsistent with truth.

Hide - Show

All is known in one-mind. All is shown in one-mind.

I expect to see that which I have created in secret to be revealed in the outer world of experience.

There is nothing to hide. I cannot hide my presence from the world. I cannot hide that which I have dwelled upon in the temple of my inner world for it always enters into my world of experience.

I dwell my attention only upon that which I prefer to experience. I turn my attention to only that which is beautiful, organized, intelligent, and grand.

In my inner experience I feel only those sensations that are pleasurable to me because I know such sensations become my actions.

I release all concepts of shame, condemnation, judgment, criticism, and punishment. I release all concepts of inferiority, bigotry, and otherness.

I expect to experience the fruit of my true nature which is elegant, wise, graceful, and gentle.

I express the qualities of my true nature and immediately experience them in my inner world.

Hopeless - Persist

The ever present intelligent power of my being always persists, moves, continues, expands, and enters into every place in all creative thought.

The arrangement of my mind reveals this fact in my world. My experiences reflect this fact in my world.

I feel endless animating power.

I sense and receive into the temple of my inner world new ideas and thoughts that contain perfect patterns seeking expression through the instrument I call my physical body.

The power of my being is always moving, stops moving, nor ends.

The power of my being moves in all places in one-mind expresses itself, in all manners of perfect expression, and is in perfect accomplishment at all stages of experience.

Hurried - Present

I am present and at ease. I am present. I am at the right place at the right time. My entire world reflects this fact. I have already done what is required to be here. I do in due time what comes next. I go through my experiences with a present ease of feeling and serenity now.

I feel at ease throughout my entire body. I am present in my body. My body feels balanced, calm, and steady. I am grounded in the present moment.

I go at a leisurely pace. I live a life of leisure.

All that I do is an immediate effect of my mood. I feel calm and stillness of mind. My body breathes easily and steadily. I feel accomplished, satisfied, and self-existent.

I go through life at an easy, present pace. Present in being, I flow freely from one moment to the next. Like the plants of the earth, the birds in the air, and the fish in the sea, the pace of my world moves with the pace of oneness. I feel the pace of oneness and I am synchronized with the heartbeat of the origin.

Each day, I progress. Each day, the arrangement of my mind grows. Everything I do is in harmony with the perfect pace of the origin of all experience.

My awareness is in sync with the timing of the origin of seasons. I move in harmony with the seasons. Because of this awareness, I know when it is the right time to start an activity and when to stop. I know when to remain observant. I know when to act. I know when to seize an opportunity and when to say no. I am always perfectly on time. I am ready when I need to be. I am prepared each day. I am ready each day.

Each day is self-contained. I am satisfied with what I have experienced today. I will be satisfied with what I experience tomorrow. I always do my best and I am proud of my activity today. I am grateful that I could experience today.

I
Ignore - Supported

I feel oneness supporting me, caring for me, providing for me, and encouraging me in all manners.

I feel an intimate connection with all through the shared connection that unites us all.

I feel the guidance of the one-mind moving through all.

I feel the creative intelligence of the one-mind expressing itself through all.

I feel at one with all vital forms of intelligence.

I accept the acts of kindness from all in my experience.

I move with the redirection and reorientation of events and conditions that guide me on the path of self-realization.

Impatient - Glad

I am glad. A path exists for me. My road is clear and all obstacles are cleared away by the largess of my present.

I am free of all obstacles and mental traps. The arrangement of my mind is congruent with truth which clarifies every experience to reveal the underlying word.

My attention is dynamic and can go to the end of any fulfilled desire. I see myself in liberty. I use my imaginal faculties in the correct method and manner which provides for me immediate resolution in all matters.

I am glad in all ways. I am glad in all conditions. I am glad to be existent, present, and aware.

I gravitate to my good. I move in the right direction because my attention is always oriented and in alignment with the origin of all satisfaction.

I am satisfied. I feel my fullness of being. I am complete. I see ideas to their completion and complete their fullest expression. What is my good belongs to me and yet the goodness of my good is shared with and benefits all in some way.

Creative intelligence knows the proper fulfillment of my good and I am intuitively directed towards the fulfillment of my good.

I am glad when I embark upon new experiences that create a wonderful journey.

I enjoy each new experience and gladly fulfill my role, the role that I have chosen for myself.

Impotent - Successful

I am successful. My power moves to deliver immediately, quickly, and effectively.

The power of my being does what I command it to do with all manner of congruency.

I succeed in all manners of expression.

I am thrilled to know that the one-mind hears me, recognizes me, and provides for me.

I feel my fulfillment, satisfaction, and delight. I am pleased. I revel in the accomplishment of my word. I succeed in experiencing all that I create in my imagination.

I feel the exhilaration that anything I imagine is possible. My faith is knowing that I create with my imagination and that all the power of my being moves to create the corresponding form in my world.

I know that I can direct attention to affirm that I can experience what delights me, be the best and truthful version of myself, do wonderful works, day after day, moment to moment, ceaselessly, eternally, and wondrously without fail.

I feel and am therefore cognizant of the wonder, greatness, and magnitude of my being. I am successful.

I am enormous in my gravity. I am creative in my impulses. I am unassailable, invincible, and unstoppable. I always prevail in the accomplishment of truth.

I am happy being as I am, living as I am, and acting as I am. I express who I am totally and completely with unadulterated joy.

I am creative intelligence. I am powerful and move my attention in any direction I please. With these characteristics in mind, I am certain to accomplish whereto I send myself in imagination.

Imagination is the realm of mind and from this realm of my being I birth all manner of life and experience.

Inactive - Moving

The one-mind is always moving. The universe is always moving and everything in it is expanding, growing, changing, evolving, and increasing in awareness of oneness.

Movement is intelligent presence in motion. Therefore, all action I experience in my world is the movement of the intelligent presence of the one-mind expressing the perfect pattern of oneness.

Oneness is the power that brings all qualities together. Oneness is the intelligence by which form is mirrored.

I feel the power of my being going forth and bringing the qualities that form my good together. I see the one-mind in action through the instrument I call my physical body and fulfill it in my outer world.

I know that my world is moving in alignment with the perfect pattern of oneness.

I see improvements everywhere I direct my attention. I do not doubt the completion of my good. I do not wonder or worry about the plans for the fulfillment of my good. I affirm in full expectation and acceptance of my good. I am aware of the plans for the fulfillment of my good. I see, hear, and visualize my good in its ripeness.

I am at ease in knowing that the power of the one-mind moves throughout the entire universe and through all distinct self-aware parties in the one-mind for the fulfillment and expression of my good.

I am relieved. I am at ease. I am quiet, steady, and calm. The power of my being is intelligent, creative, dedicated to achieving ever greater vistas of knowledge.

Ever at work, the power of my being always succeeds. I succeed while I am awake. I succeed while I sleep. I succeed in all places where the power of my being precedes in imagination.

Inadequate - Overflowing

There exists no boundaries, obstructions, and limitations separating me from my good.

All that is my good is inherent in me.

All that is my good exists entirely within the power and presence of my being.

The power and presence of my being is universal, unlimited, intelligent, creative, boundless, and infinite. The origin of all good bears the fruit of goodness, wholeness, peace, and superfluent abundance of diverse expression through me and into my experience.

I feel the goodness of my being overflowing into my outer world.

I sense the joy of my being and allow the fullest expression of the quality of my true nature.

I dissolve all limitations of attention. I dissolve all adherence to superstitious habits of thought. I dissolve all belief in limitations and externally caused constraints.

The power of my being breaks down all false structures. The simplicity inherent in the power of my being unifies all constructive thought to build a world of harmony, beauty, and overflowing light.

Incapable - Master

I am the master of my mood.

I am the master of my feeling capacity.

I am the master of my imagination.

I am the master of my movements.

I am the master of my habits.

I am the master of my responses.

I am the master of the words I speak.

I am the master of the choices I make.

I am the master of my health. I alone use the instrument I call my physical body.

In the consideration of all these faculties and the position I hold I use them with the power of my entire being.

I am the master of what I create in my imagination. I am the master of my choices.

I choose to orient my attention to the truth of my nature. Or, I may reject the truth of my nature.

I may engage the power of my being in the fulfillment of my nature. Or, I may engage the power of my being in the creation of an external power, a separate self, and the deception that what exists in my outer world is the controlling law and master of all my mental faculties.

There is no mind beyond the one-mind. In oneness, I am connected and part and parcel. I have a permanent, enduring, everlasting connection to the one-mind which knows and personally supports me in the fulfillment of my good.

With the power of my being I navigate the creation of my inner experience by the decisive use of my mental faculties. No force may stop me from this use for it is my nature, inherent to all.

Incompatible - Match

My outer world of experience matches my inner world of experience.

I fully understand the effects of my thinking. I create that which I command in the depths of my inner world of creation.

I use my imagination - the womb of my creative ability - to construct beautiful images of those experiences, relationships, and feelings that I find acceptable to me.

I dwell upon imaginal acts in ease, clarity, and vividness. I experience with exactness and attention to detail that which I seek to experience in the outer world.

I dedicate my power of being towards the expression of good in my experience. I curate experiences that ever increase in excellence and expansion.

It feels natural to create imaginal designs that best outpicture visions of harmony, oneness, togetherness, and perfection.

I feel united with my good. I feel the presence of my good through my connection to the one-mind. I sense all glory available to me within the presence of my being to express and experience at all times.

I feel connected, surrounded, embraced, and appreciated. I feel the vastness of the one-mind and all parties to whom I share a common connection.

Incomplete - Accomplished

All is accomplished. There is nothing to accomplish. All exists as completed states of being.

My only remaining task is to enter into the state of completion through experience.

Experience is presence. To be present is to experience. Without presence there is no experience.

Without the power of my being there is no now from which to experience the fullness of my being.

Thus, all experience exists readily available to me *in* my true nature and the true me is part and parcel with all in one-mind.

I am aligned in full attention to the origin of all experience. In this direct connection I enter into any experience with my mental faculties. I feel the completed qualities of all thoughts. I touch with my feeling capacities perfect forms of thought. In this unification with perfect thoughtforms I intuitively, instinctively know their innate knowledge.

Through this knowing I experience the fullness of expression of perfect thoughtforms. With the instrument I call my physical body I amplify and magnify perfect thoughtforms reflected into my outer world.

In oneness, I am infinitely whole. In oneness, I am changeless. In oneness, I am eternal. I release the illusion of change. I release the illusion of death. I release the illusion of separation, division, and externalities. There is only oneness. There is only accomplishment. There is only fulfillment in all forms.

Indigestion - Breath

I expand the arrangement of my mind to correspond to the expansion of my understanding of my true nature.

I recognize the expansion and grandeur of my being. I accept my true nature and act in harmony with my inherent capacities to imagine and experience new, diverse forms of perfection.

I release incompatible habits of thinking that do not accomplish all forms of excellence.

I release attitudes that have kept me from fully experiencing and materializing my good in the outer world of experience.

I allow the creative intelligent presence of the one-mind to move freely throughout the instrument I call my physical body. I release myself from mental traps that confined my attention to false constructions of thought.

I leave behind old habits and orient my attention to the full breadth of behavior that would assist me in expressing perfect moods.

I always progress in a perfect sequence of accomplishment in all experiences. I recognize the perfection and completion in every experience. Every experience is an accomplishment of a fully expressed idea felt in the power of my being.

Every moment is a glorification of a beautiful idea. Every moment is an opportunity to feel the connection we all share as one.

I let go of all constraining thoughts. I attune my attention to the good within me and within all.

I appreciate who I am. I feel gratitude for all that exists within the power of my being and for the fact that I am able to experience myself in individuation.

Inferior - Exceptional

The only thoughts that I permit to enter into the temple of my inner world are thoughts from the origin of all perfect forms.

I impress upon the power of my being perfect patterns of thought. In my imagination I envision all manners of excellence in all completed forms.

I attune my attention to speak of the good inherent in all. I attune my attention to recognize excellence in all forms and manners of expression.

I act according to my true nature which is excellent, graceful, intelligent, creative and poised. I direct the faculties of my mind correctly to express the beauty of my true nature. I employ my imagination to experience the fulfillment of wondrous scenes of accomplishment.

I complete all tasks with an attitude of excellence. I bring attention to the capacities of the intelligent, creative power that is endowed in all.

I attribute every successful experience and every feeling of satisfaction to the creative intelligence that is the one-mind of which I am part and parcel.

I pursue activities that express my natural qualities of being. I allow my body-mind to freely express my true nature.

I am distinguished and honored in one-mind. I see myself expressing all manner of grace and elegance.

Inflexible - Elastic

My attention is elastic. I easily direct my attention to new concepts that increase my understanding and connection to the origin of all experience.

I move freely and easily through experience. My experience flows from me and because of this form follows the function I direct my power to express.

I move from one world to another with ease. I direct my attention to any experience I want to join. I shift my mood to access a new world of thought and experience. In mere moments, I create a new imaginal experience that will surely come to expression in the realm of form.

I create a new conception of my persona through which I see the events of my life reflecting my new role. I play any role I find acceptable and I perform the tasks of this role with ease. The power in me transforms my present self concept into any conception I choose. I am whoever I decide to be. I accomplish anything I decide to experience. I can see myself through the eyes of others as I would like to be.

With my imagination, I perceive myself through any mind because each distinct self-aware part of the one-mind is connected to the one-mind. How I see myself is how all in my experience see me. With great clarity, admiration, and oneness I see myself with esteem. I am known in one-mind as an integral, essential, important part of the whole.

I understand everything. I can do anything. My attention through which I direct my power is elastic, moveable, and unlimited. I can go to infinite places and experience infinitely. I am free and liberated. I cannot be held down or held back. I only make progress. I am everlasting, unwavering power experiencing itself through individuated self-awareness.

Injure - Intact

I am intact. I am whole.

Nothing that ever appears to happen to me, nor false conditions can deceive me into believing that I am any less whole or reduced by my experiences.

I can never be and was never reduced by my experiences.

I cannot be made smaller, less than, or made incomplete by conditions of mind or of the outer world.

No behavior based on false thoughts can break me down or tear me apart. I am and will always be intact for I come from wholeness and oneness.

I am oneness experiencing myself.

I am wholeness experiencing myself.

I am intelligent power aware of myself.

No thought is bigger than the power that I am. No thought has power over me.

All experiences show me the orientation of my attention and the arrangement of my mind. I am free from false suggestions that attempt to distract my attention. I am free from doubt of the origin of my being. I know who I am, my origin, and everlasting wholeness.

I enter into awareness of the wholeness that is my experience. My experience is wholesome, complete, and excellent.

I feel the fullness of my being. I feel the completion of my power. I feel the perfection and infinity of my life force.

I never walk alone because I am always in the presence of the one-mind. I am intimately, perfectly known and appreciated in oneness. I feel my connection to the one-mind and to all.

I am still. I am centered. I am stable and firmly planted in the stability and foundation of the one-mind.

Insanity - Purity

I sense my connection to the origin of all perfect thought.

Perfect patterns of thought emanate in the presence of my being for I am part and parcel of the one-mind which is the center and source of perfection.

I perceive with my mind's eye and feel within the depths of my inner world the perfect power of my being.

My mind is quiet, still, centered, and firmly rooted in thoughts of truth and beauty.

My mental environment is clean, organized, and structured after perfection.

I sense perfect forms. I recognize perfect patterns of thought and generate thoughtforms modeled after perfection and purity in my mind.

There is no external mind. There exists no external power. I release my attention from all false and deceptive thinking. I hold onto goodness. I affix my attention to the oneness of being.

I sense perfect harmony and organization within the instrument I call my physical body. I feel joy, clarity, and enthusiastic pleasure of being.

I abandon all false powers and authority. I turn my attention to the everlasting intelligent presence of my being.

I recall moments of oneness in my experience. I feel surrounded by parties who express unconditional appreciation for me. I feel kindness encompassing me and surrounding me.

Insecure - Stable

Every aspect of the arrangement of my mind is founded upon the foundation of truth.

The entire arrangement of my mind is firmly grounded upon the immutable fact that I am part and parcel with the one-mind.

No false thought can dissuade me from the confidence of my true character.

No aggression, no threat of violence, no rumor of disaster can prevent me from dwelling in perfect serenity.

I think only of the beautiful. I imagine scenes of ever greater majesty. I feel after only that which is acceptable to me.

I expect success in all endeavors of creation.

I move steadily. I think clearly. I speak affirmatively of the good that exists within me.

All of my affairs are stable in progression. All of my activities are coordinated in perfect organization.

Insolvent - Funded

I am funded.

I fund large expenses easily and immediately. I have the funds available to purchase items of all prices. All purchases are small purchases. I have funds on hand and immediately available to me.

I have my own funds and never need to borrow. I am my own bank and fund my projects. I have funds available to me in my bank account, my home, and in my pockets. I never leave home without sufficient amounts of funding and currency.

I have all sorts of funding available to me. I have exactly what is required to make an exchange of goods or services. I can never outspend myself. I never waste money. Every purchase I make is an investment and I invest wisely. Everything and everyone who receives money, currency, or value of any kind from me prospers. I am prospering now.

I never need to wait for my good. I have it now. I have funding now. There is nothing keeping me from my good and from accomplishing my goals. I always have the funding I require. I always have funds with me and available to me in my home, in my bank account, and in other places. I never live without funding. I always have funds. I always have more funds than I need. I have funds of all kinds growing and multiplying.

Funds are multiplying in my experience. I have an ever increasing supply of funding. I always have funds. I have unlimited funding to do with as I please.

I have more assets than liabilities. My assets increase my money. I acquire assets and funding easily. I manage my funds and assets with ease and joy. I am given funds and assets and maximize their value and benefit to myself and others quickly and efficiently.

I am fully funded. My projects are fully funded. I have funding. I fund my dreams. I fund my projects. I can fund anything I like. I will always be funded. I was always funded. There is no limit to my funding.

Insufficient - Superfluent

I am superfluent. I have more than enough of everything. I produce so much value that I give what extra I have away to further expand the value and joy in my experience.

I have so much abundance that I use my abundance however I choose. I never lose, waste, or squander the abundance of resources in my possession for, through me, my abundance goes to the right destinations and further multiplies.

Abundance overflows into my experience. I have extra to share. I feel abundance in my stores. In my storehouses of supply, I have an outpouring of resources that ceaselessly enters into my experience. I channel extra abundance into the experiences of others so they may, too, know this feeling of superfluency.

I share my wealth of resources to add to my experience. I recognize an increase everywhere I go and in everything I do. My resources always overflow and I direct these resources to their intended destination.

I am an open channel of wealth in my experience. I see myself as wealthy. I see myself as prosperous. I see myself succeeding in all my experiences. I am invested in profitable endeavors. I surpass all expectations. I have extra. I am aware of the extra that I have.

I know what to do with my superfluency. I know how to use what extra I have. Nature shows me that it is superfluous. Thus, I am, too. With joy, I embrace my abundance of being. I bring my abundance into my experience.

Insulted - Honored

I am honored. I honor myself. I know my worth and I sense my own integrity. I alone determine my own value and qualities. I describe myself with kind words and I know who I am. I know myself better than anyone else because the origin of all personality directly informs me of my perfect heritage.

Noone in a deceptive mood tells me who I am, what I can do, or what I can experience. Nobody, besides me, has the power to determine my life experiences. Nobody has power over me. The everlasting power dwells in me and I send it out to fulfill my word.

I have control over my experiences and I freely speak in honor of myself.

I recognize my contributions. I remember all the good I have created throughout my life. I recognize my own, inherent worth and grow in awareness of it daily. I deliberately create experiences that affirm how good I feel about myself, others, and all of life.

I honor others with my presence just as they honor me with theirs. I feel the wonder of all interactions at their perfectly appointed hour. I clearly recognize how life honors me. I accept all that is good and perfect and I delight in such experiences.

I cast out all doubt, lies, and deceptive thinking with bravery and strength of spirit. I stand tall, poised, and firm as I affirm my integrity, value, and character. I decide what I believe is true and I only affirm and live by truth.

Interrupt - Connect

I am in perfect harmony with the one-mind. I constantly reorganize the arrangement of my mind in greater likeness of the one-mind.

The instrument I call my physical body is the perfect arrangement of my mind intently attuned to the emanations of the one-mind.

I am totally and completely free. My attention is freed from all deceptive thinking. My subconscious mind is the reflection of an acceptance and awareness of all truth.

My attention is connected to the one-mind and therefore my imagination constructs imaginal designs that express the truth that enters into it.

I am entirely aligned with the origin of all power. I feel the power of my being pulsating through my entire experience. My mind is renewed, restored, and revitalized with the expansive, all present power of the one-mind. I feel the invigorating power dwelling in me. Every part of my body-mind is perfected as a result of a direct connection with all intelligent, creative self-aware power.

I am perfectly placed. I am perfectly poised. I am aligned and at ease. I am flexible and boundaryless. I am circulating freely and ever expanding. I am directly oriented towards my good and it is expressed in my experience.

J
Jealousy - Appreciation

All are inherently valuable in one-mind.

All are capable of expressing creative intelligence for all are creatively intelligent.

I feel with my mental faculties the creativity and intelligence that all express. I recognize the talents all possess. I understand the value and use of all talents.

I use my talents in a constructive manner. I feel the connection that all share through the expression of the true self through all means of expression.

I recognize my own inherent talents. I recognize my own creative tendencies and use the power of my being to bring unifying ideas into experience.

I feel a rejuvenating enthusiasm circulating in my inner world.

I feel a light, effervescent joy emanating from the instrument I call my physical body.

There is no obstructive, divisive thinking in my mind. I release all thoughts of doubt, worry, and exhaustion and replace them with feelings of easy, superfluous, and unending creativity.

K
Kill - Preserve

The power of my being preserves all and contains all. The power of my being sustains all, gives form and shape to the diverse patterns of intelligence. The power in me honors itself and all diverse expressions of truth for we are all one in one-mind.

The one-mind is suitable and hospitable for all manner of creation. My entire world is suitable, acceptable, and hospitable for me to move, play, and express my good.

My body-mind is safe, secure, pleasant and designed for me to experience my own world in peace, tranquility, and harmony.

The power of my being preserves all living truth because the one-mind is everlasting, continual, immutable, imperishable living truth and is entirely self-sustaining.

There is no other power or force in the universe. All that is contained in the universe is subject to the power and truth that is the one-mind. All that is contained in my visible world is subject to my command.

There is no threat to my integrity. There is no danger to my wholeness. There is no harm, word, or activity that can destroy, alter, or disempower the truth of my nature. No party may commit that which I do not approve according to the fulfillment of my good. No party may be outside of the will of the one-mind in my world. All minds in my world are oriented and directed by the one-mind in the completion of my good.

All in my world are directed and instructed with plans of loving fulfillment. I am safe, I am whole, I am preserved in the presence of the one-mind. I am treasured.

L
Lack - Content

Nothing is lacking in my experience. There is no emptiness. There is no absence. Everything is available to me in my experience. All resources are present.

What I see or do not see in my outer experience does not account for the vastness of my inner world. Nor does the outer world of form tell me who I am; only the expression of my thoughts and those of others.

I direct my attention and the power of my being on those forms I intend to bring into my experience. No one can do this but the power in me.

I feel strong in my ability to create designs in my imagination. It is easy and natural for me for I am self-aware creative intelligence endowed with the power to construct forms with the direction of my attention and inner sensations.

I am complete and thus content in who I am. I feel the power of my being exuding into my outer experience. In me is the content of all experiences. In me exists everything I could possibly desire and imagine. In me is the animating power to give expression. I have everything I need because I have it all in the power of my being.

Noone can take away from me. Noone can control what is mine. Noone can control where I direct my attention. I only consent my attention to the good, the lovely, and of good report.

Every day, in every way, I am content and fulfilled.

Lament - Triumphant

I am triumphant. I succeed in all endeavors to which I engage my power of being.

I am ready and capable of the fulfillment of my good.

I enjoy the conscious experience of the power of my being.

I permanently dwell in the grandeur, serenity, and perfection of oneness which perpetuates feelings of completion, wholeness, and fulfillment.

All is achieved. All is finished. All is whole.

I actively and continually experience achievement, completion, and wholeness in every experience.

The tasks set out before me are merely experiences of organized expressions of fulfillment.

Each moment is complete. Each experience is whole.

I continue on eternally from one glory to the next.

There is nothing to achieve.

There is nothing to create.

There is only fulfillment through expression of perfection.

Limited - Undeniable

I am undeniable. I do not deny my origin. I do not deny the power of my being. I do not deny what I am capable of creating. I do not deny how far my power can go to create for me causeways for the expression of my good. I do not deny my good.

I do not deny the supremacy of the instructions by which my good is ordered to be fulfilled through me. I do not deny my intuitive connection to the origin of all intelligent creative thought. I do not deny my capacity to use my imagination to construct images that are beautiful, expansive, and helpful for my fullest expression of being.

I do not deny my nature as an intelligent, creative awareness expressing oneself through the instrument that I call my physical body for the creation of my world.

I do not deny good from entering into my mind and the temple of my being. I accept the entirety of my good and the truth of my true identity into my mind.

Because I always accept myself, I am undeniable to the rest of the world. Doors are opened for me. Paths are made for me. Places are reserved for me. The power of my being opens a way for me everywhere I go.

I always find what I seek to understand. I always touch what I feel after. I always know what I wonder. I always get what I reach for.

I accept myself and I am accepted everywhere I go. I approve of myself and hear this affirmed in my world. I belong to the unity of the one-mind and thus belong in my world in every circumstance and in every event I find unfolding in my experience.

I am empowered to go in the direction of my good. I always have what is required in the fulfillment of my good.

Lost - Oriented

I know who I am.

I am part and parcel with the one-mind. I share with all an infinite, unbreakable connection to the origin of perfection, creativity, intelligence, and knowing. This connection is the power of my presence.

I turn my attention to the power of my presence and I feel with my sensing faculties the wisdom, understanding, and ideas that are always available to me.

I feel all that is good in my inner temple of being. I feel the joy of knowing my true self. I feel the pleasure of orienting my attention to the pleasure of my being.

It feels good to be me. It feels good to experience myself. Because of this all feel good around me. I feel comfortable within the presence of my being and as such all feel comfortable around me.

I focus my attention on the goodness inherent in me. I recognize the goodness inherent in me. I am and have always been endowed with unending creative intelligent power because that is who I am at my nature.

I recognize every moment that I accept a thought in my inner world and impress it upon the power of my being. I recognize my natural imaginative abilities and organize new, creative experiences to enjoy.

My experience of self-knowing allows me to understand and participate in all manner of creative expression. All is accomplished and complete in one-mind and I am able to enjoy everything in ceaseless oneness.

Lust - Satisfied

The one-mind satisfies all.

The one-mind satisfies all questions.

The one-mind creative endeavors.

I am satisfied through communion with feeling the qualities of the ideal mood I decide to experience.

I enter into any experience when I turn my attention to the source of all experience. I turn my attention to my imagination and meet the experience I intend to create. I cannot fail in the satisfaction of my decisions.

In self-determining propulsion, the power of my being is the power through which animation is possible. The power of my being is the force that satisfies what has yet to be satisfied.

There are countless experiences and I may experience anyone I choose.

All I do is direct my attention to the one-mind through my imagination and construct an experience with my imaginal senses and send forth my power to organize my outer world to the completion of this act. Through this organization of creative power I satisfy my nature as creative intelligence.

I am creative intelligence growing in strength, expanding in awareness, and partnering with every known self-aware part of the one-mind.

I cannot fail in the satisfaction of this truth.

I am satisfied through oneness.

All is one. I am a part of all. All is in my power of being.

M
Manipulate - Attract

I feel the wholeness of my being. I sense my connection with all good through the power of my being.

I enjoy the goodness I feel in me. I allow myself to express the joy in me.

The power of my being directs my attention to focus on perfect forms.

I come into contact with all that corresponds to my nature. I act according to my true nature. I recognize all that reflects the beauty, grandeur, elegance, and wholeness of oneness.

I enjoy the fullness of my being. I enjoy being who I naturally am.

All that serves to fulfill my good comes together perfectly and in perfect sequence.

I feel goodness in every experience and recognize the unfolding of my good at each perfect phase of completion.

I direct my attention to only the power of my being on which is my good and expect to experience only that which is acceptable to me.

All experiences come together perfectly for me. All events reflect the perfect pattern of thought emanating from the origin of all creation.

Murder - Protect

I am strong. I am centered in the strength and power of my being.

The one-mind preserves, protects, and reorients all at all times.

I am secure in the presence of my being.

My mind is clear.

My attention is focused entirely upon the voice and instructions of the one-mind.

I have integrity. The true me can never be hurt. The true me can never be destroyed.

I release all thoughts of division, separation, threat, injury, and pain. I orient my attention upon unity, connection, wholeness, and eternal power.

I am embodied with the intelligence of one-mind.

I walk in grandeur. I walk in alignment with all power. I walk in possession of the truth.

I move in perfect harmony in the preservation of wholeness. I am contained in the continual presence of being.

N

Numb - Sensation

I sense the power of my being. I sense the purity, pulsation, and unending vitality of the power available to me at all times.

I sense with all clarity of mind. I reach any mental design in one-mind with my attention.

I observe in simple understanding any form to which I direct my attention.

I activate my imagination to explore any structure of thought. I can touch any form and understand its intended purpose.

I direct my attention with intention and thus create in my imagination an experience that is sure to pass from my inner world to my outer world of experience.

I correct all false thinking. I correct all misuse of imagination. I dissolve all false thoughtforms. I dissolve all false conditions of mind.

False conditions fade in my presence. From the passing of experience flows new structures of thought. All conditions pass away. I remain in the eternal presence of being.

I sense the perfecting presence of the one-mind as a quality of my true nature. This perfecting presence upon which I cast my attention immediately unfolds new patterns of thought in my imagination and reinvigorates the total arrangement of my mind in fullness of perfection. I renew the total arrangement of my mind by dwelling in my perfect presence of being.

Numbness - Pulsation

I feel the heartbeat of oneness. I feel the pulsation of the one-mind gently sending animating waves of vitality through the instrument I call my physical body.

I feel my physical body revitalizing, reorganizing, and stabilizing in harmony with the pulsation of the one-mind.

I feel the gentle flow of pure thought streaming through my body's communication channels. My attention is firmly rooted in attention centered on stillness of mind.

My mind is clear of all false thinking. All false thought forms dissolve away in my mind. I feel the nourishment that oneness brings to every aspect of my mental atmosphere.

There is no other power that can control my quality of experience. There is no false thoughtform that can distract me from experiencing the qualities of my true nature.

I breathe in comfort. I breathe in the deepness of connection with all. I feel goodness circulating in my mental atmosphere.

I feel joy, pleasure, and superfluent integrity in all aspects of being.

I rest in a perfect state of being. I dwell in the comfort of everlasting purity.

I am easy. I am complete. I am accomplished in one-mind. All is well.

0
Obsese - Rejuvenate

The power of my being stimulates all change in form in my outer world of experience.

The power of my being cannot be conformed to false images without my consent.

The power of my being cannot be limited to false patterns of thought without my acceptance.

There is no external mind or power that determines my appearance in the outer world.

I am the master of my mind.

I am the master of my mood.

I am the master of the forms I construct in my imagination.

I am the master of the power of my being which I use for the perfect fulfillment of my true nature.

I see the instrument I call my physical body with loving eyes.

I see into the mirror of my outer experience with loving eyes.

I see only the perfection of the one mind of which I am part and parcel. I accept my true nature. I accept who I am through diverse expressions of form.

I feel the goodness of my being. I move my physical body in harmony with the one-mind. There is no one else I desire to be but the true me.

I see myself in my true form. I accept my true form.

Obstruction - Direct

I am directly connected to the greatest and only power by which life is formed.

There is no other source of creation. There is no other creative force. All is born from the power of the one intelligent, creative mind that I am part and parcel.

Nothing can take away my direct connection to the one creative intelligent mind. Because this is an unchangeable fact, I always receive a rejuvenating understanding of my fundamental state of being as intelligent power.

Nothing obstructs my light; not even the shadows of deceptive thought. There are no shadows present in the effervescent glow of my own being. Thus, I can uncreate and make disappear any unacceptable form that obscures my vision of my true self.

There exists no middleman between me and the power, care, and embrace of the one-mind.

I am aware of my existence as a part and parcel of the one-mind.

I am creative, intelligent, and transformative self-aware power recognized with distinction in the whole that is the one-mind.

Oppose - Surrender

I surrender all present limitations. I surrender all present misconceptions. I surrender all false thoughtforms that once obscured my awareness of the truth.

I surrender to a new reality in which I am free of all past deceptions. I enter into a new life and a new order of mind. I experience a new self-conception that is liberated from constricting thoughts. I allow myself to be the best version of my true self. I accept experiences that best fulfill my good.

I release all thoughts that oppose the fulfillment of my good. I release the power of my being from the patterns of false thinking. I release constraints that I placed upon my mind. My mind is free from the shadows of present conditions and I enter into events and circumstances that reveal the fulfillment of my good.

The time is now to enter into a new manner of expression. I am completely restored to my connection with the one-mind. My attention is solely oriented to the feelings of satisfaction that my good has come together and is now complete.

I receive intelligent patterns that flow from true thoughts. I receive mental images, concepts, and feelings that strengthen the concentration of my power in the immediate fulfillment of my good.

I am free in every way. I accept the revelatory power of truth. I express myself in accordance with the fulfillment of my good.

I now witness the unfolding of my good in the outer world. The experiences that I have chosen are now revealed in the outer world of form. What was once an unformed idea is now accepted fact. I completed my assumption of the fulfilled thought. The power of my being accepts the new reality now as it is finished. The origin of experience lives through me and brings forth completion through me.

Every thought, action, and word confirms the completion of my good. Events affirm the completion of my good as the outer world surrenders to the authority of my mind.

Oppressed - Great

I feel the entirety and expanse of the power of my being.

I feel my personal, intimate connection with the one-mind.

I have eternal access to all power in one-mind through this unbreakable connection that I share with all.

I feel and recognize the dignity, excellence, intelligence of the presence in me. I turn to this power at all times. I orient my attention to the origin of my nature.

I express my true nature unceasingly.

I constructin my imagination imaginal designs that reflect the greatness available to me in the power of my being.

There is no external power or force that can oppress the unlimited, expansive, boundless presence that I am. There is no authority that stops me from exercising my perfect mental faculties to create new pathways and experiences that facilitate the fulfillment of my true nature.

The power of my being can not be constrained, imprisoned, contained, limited, bounded, and minimized.

I direct my attention to any place in one-mind. I direct my attention to focus on the wealth of beauty and perfection within the oneness that pervades everything.

I observe with expectation the fulfillment of my good each day. I am delighted, overjoyed, and pleased to witness the accomplishment of my good in every experience through all manner of creative, intelligent expression.

Oppression - Expansion

The power of my being is limitless.

The power of my being cannot be contained, held back, retained, conformed, or minimized.

The power of my being is vast, infinite, unlimited and fulfilling.

My understanding of my true nature is ever expanding. My understanding of my inherent capacities and my unlimited mental faculties is always increasing.

My attention cannot be limited or contained. My attention can travel over vast distances and enter into any intended moment.

I witness the fulfillment of all good. I enter into the accomplishment of all perfect designs.

There is no external mind. There is no external design. There is no external power that keeps me from the fulfillment of my good and the complete understanding of my true nature.

No false thought or illusion separates me from my true nature. I always orient my attention and feeling faculties to the one-mind.

In oneness I feel the expanse of the oneness. I feel the connection I share with all distinct self-aware parts of the one-mind. There is no division. There is no separation. There is only one.

No imaginal act, or temporary condition formed in my own personal experience can distract my attention from the expanse of my being.

I reorient my attention into oneness with the one-mind. I recalibrate my inner feelings to sense the presence of the one-mind and the vast intelligence inherent in me. I redirect my mind to reproduce the perfect pattern of thoughts emanating from the one-mind.

There is no condition that detains me. There is no party who controls me. There is no limitation that stops me.

The power of my being is vast, powerful, magnanimous, and overrules all false thoughts. I accept the truth of my nature and release all false assumptions.

I am free in all manner of expression and in all experiences.

Outraged - Firm

I am grand. My mind is solidly rooted in the power of my being. As such, I am calm, collected, centered, and at one with the one-mind.

The power of my being cannot be severed from oneness.

No person, no condition, nor false thinking moves me from my true place. All is well. I cannot be swept up in the tide of sensations stirred by false thoughts.

I orient my attention permanently in the direction of truth. I am unbothered by murmurs of false ideas. I give no sustaining power to false thoughtforms.

The power of my being is sustaining power. Truth, goodness, and everlasting power sustains me.

I remained undisturbed, tranquil, and silent. My attention focuses on the stillness of my being.

I turn my attention to my good and what is now available to me. I release what was into memory and now hold my attention fixedly upon my present experience. I see what is available to me now. I feel the direction of my mind entering into a higher vista of truth.

I am impassioned by the thought of my good.

My attention is acutely and directly attuned to my good. My awareness rises above all false feelings and touches upon true knowledge of my nature.

Overwhelm - Quiet

The power of my being is calm. I feel serenity in the depth of my being.

My mind is clear. My mind is quiet.

I feel centered within the power of my being.

I feel the stillness of my being.

I hear nothing but natural sounds.

I hear only comforting words. I feel the comfort of my being.

I move with great ease. I delight in the simplicity of my being.

I feel the expanse of oneness.

I feel steady. I feel unity.

I feel stable in the strength and poise of oneness.

All is well.

All is one.

Overwhelmed - Magnanimous

The power of my being is unstoppable. There is no limit to the power of my being. I no longer chain down the power in me. I no longer restrict my attention to slavish, subjected thinking habits.

I express freedom. I express unlimited power. The power of my being breaks down all barriers of awareness. I direct my attention to accomplish a task and the power of my being fulfills the completion of my good.

The power of the one-mind in me is unstoppable. As a function of being connected and part and parcel of the one-mind, all that I enter into oneness with yields to the power of my being.

I claim peace. I claim authority over all conditions in my world. I claim sovereignty over my mind and the instrument I call my physical body. I declare myself free from all limited thoughts and assumptions.

Everything is accomplished by the power of the one-mind. I direct the power of my being with the concentration of my attention on that which I seek the state of oneness.

In all its magnificence, perfection, intelligent creative capacity, the power of my being that is the one-mind flows through my body-mind to accomplish all plans.

The power of my being working through me cannot fail. I obey the instructions of the fulfillment of my good with exact accuracy and in ripeness. There is nothing to do but to fulfill.

There is nothing to get for all is gathered. There is nothing to achieve for all is done. There is only to experience and to enter into experience.

I am magnanimous. All yields to the power of my being that is the one-mind. The total arrangement of my mind yields to the power of the one-mind and obeys commands regardless of what it accepts as true.

The one-mind causes all forms to bow down to the supremacy and dominance of the power and presence that emanates in all directions.

I will never again be controlled by false feelings, false thoughtforms, false suggestions, and talks of fearful image makers. All such efforts and forms dissolve in the power and presence of the one-mind in me.

I will never again deceive myself into believing that I am limited. I am unlimited, expanded, boundless, great, and whole.

I am part and parcel of the one-mind. I reject all false illusions of division, separation, and otherness.

All is one. All is known in one-mind.

Oneness is the solution for all matters. Oneness is the manner of all accomplishment. Oneness is the achievement of all good. Oneness is the entrance to liberation. Oneness is health.

In oneness I experience the magnanimity of the one-mind.

All is accomplished in one-mind.

All is whole in one-mind. All is well in one-mind. I live and dwell in one mind. I am an instrument for the total and complete, variegated expression of the one-mind.

I am known and loved in one-mind. I am delivered in one-mind.

Oneness is the truth of my being and the pattern of my continuous expression

I am fulfilled by the one-mind. I am complete in oneness.

P
Pain - Comfort

I am comfort. I feel the calmness of my being radiating and circulating throughout my mind, through the instrument I call my physical body, and into my world.

I am a comforting force that expresses calm thoughts and feelings into my experience. I override all incongruent deceptive thinking and renew myself with relief and steadiness.

I am centered, steadfast, and large. I expand in steady streaming flows of uniform presence.

The strength of my presence is illuminating and empowering.

I uncreate all false conditions. I withdraw my attention from all temporary conditions. I focus my attention on what is everlasting and unending: the goodness and transformative power of the one-mind.

The one-mind works as me and through me to transform, rebuild, and restore all with the revitalizing power of creative intelligence.

I focus my attention on perfect images. I dwell upon perfect feelings. Oneness clarifies all obscurity. I use my words to write over present conditions.

My word command forms to reorganize into the corresponding pattern.

I am comfort. I feel comfort. I radiate comfort.

Pinch - Fill

I feel the fulfilling presence of the one-mind living and dwelling in me.

I feel the relief of all that is good circulating through the instrument I call my physical body.

I feel the expansion of intelligent power expanding every closed part of my body.

The total arrangement of my mind reflects that which is radiant, vital, and pure. I turn my attention to the qualities of mind that immediately demonstrate my power of being.

All that was closed now opening. All that was cramped is now circulating. All that was blocked is now pumping.

All that was resistant is now growing.

I recognize perfect patterns of organization and structures of thought in their original design.

I am poised.

I use my physical body correctly because I use my mental faculties correctly to express my natural state of being.

Poison - Pristine

My mind is pure because I am pure.

The instrument I call my physical body is an extension of my mind and is also pure.

I only allow pure thoughtforms and feelings into my imagination. I dwell my attention only on the pure.

As I expand my mind, I relax into a restful form. There is no strain in my mind.

There is no strain where I send my power. The power of my being goes before me to accomplish the task whereto I have sent it.

There is nothing for me to do but to send forth my power to clear the path ahead of me so that I walk in ease, comfort, and joy.

My physical body is a perfectly functioning instrument that harmonizes with the thoughts that I feed it. My physical body assimilates perfect thoughts and creates the image of what I feel so that I and all parties can witness my thoughts expressed through me.

I give attention to thoughts by animating them in imagination.

Just as I give life and form to a thought, I withdraw my power and uncreate any thought that is unacceptable to me. I can send it back from whence it came. I replace any undesirable thought and mood with a thought and mood that is desirable to me. I sit still and quiet with myself and focus my attention on the opposite mood and allow the concept of *pristine* to enter into my imagination.

I now feel pristine feelings. I see pristine images. I hear pristine thoughts.

My life is pristine because I am pristine.

I renew my mind to be a perfect reflection of the origin of all life.

The power of my being is perfect, my mind is perfect.

The arrangement of my mind is clean and pure. I feel clean and pure.

Possess - Borrow

All that is my good is for me to enjoy. The entire world of experience is for me to enjoy. All parties share in the enjoyment of all goods available to all as one.

I release all thoughts of possession. I release all thoughts of greed. I release all burdens. I release identification with objects, persons, organizations, and habits of mind.

I express the qualities of my true nature. I possess qualities of joy, enthusiasm, elation, happiness, freedom, and liberty of expression.

I borrow objects, titles, places, and spaces. All that enters into my experience is for me to enjoy and steward until the next party borrows it.

I am always happy with the objects I use to fulfill my good. I always enjoy the experiences in which I employ objects to complete the task at hand.

I steward all that is in my temporary possession and maintain until the moment to relinquish has arrived.

I manage all that is in my care with excellence. I grow all benefits from that which is under my care.

I nourish all that is in my charge with tender attention and affection. How I care for that which is in my charge reflects my qualities of integrity, organization, wisdom, and understanding.

I value all that is in my care and in my charge.

I direct the use of all that is in my care with perfect understanding.

Poverty - Fulfillment

I am fulfilled by the power of my being.

I am self-aware, intelligent power connected to the one-mind, the origin of all experience. I harness the creative power of the one-mind to form designs in my imagination.

I animate every thought that is acceptable to me. I magnify a thought with my attention until it expands throughout my entire mind. I feel a thought's form in me and sense its completion.

Creative endeavors reach completion from start to finish. I always reach the end of every imaginative design by experiencing it in the outer world of form.

All forms are contained as potential for expression in the one-mind.

I am aware of my connection to the one-mind and can always experience the fulfillment of a thought by the creation of a mood.

I am the operant power that fulfills the law of one. All is one. I know my oneness with all parts of the one-mind. I become one with anything by thinking feelingly of it until I know it in my imagination. When the thought becomes fully expressed in my imagination, I know that it will immediately express itself through me into the world of form.

I sense immediate fulfillment by the successful creation of a mood. I rest, fulfilled by the completion of my imaginative design. I move my attention in harmony with the mood I have selected to fulfill. I am satisfied in my connection with the origin of all experience. I am unlimited in experience. I fulfill all that I become one with in being.

The power of my being is ever flowing with ideas, solutions, answers. I fill the outer world of form with my imaginative designs. I express my true nature in the outer world of form.

I choose what to express. I never fail. I always prevail.

I have an eternal connection with the one-mind because I am a self-aware part of the one-mind.

Powerless - Light

I dwell in the light of the oneness. I turn my attention to the connection I share in one-mind.

I attune my attention to the origin of all inspired thought. I feel the emanating pulsation of perfect being.

I rest in the solitude, intelligence, and creativity of the oneness. I am stabled, centered, and firmly rooted in oneness with all.

I exude the intelligence of my being. I express all thoughts which I have permitted to enter into the temple of my inner world. I dwell upon perfect thoughts and amplify and express perfect patterns through the instrument I call my physical body.

The power of my being is light. I illuminate all thoughts and animate all thoughts in my outer world.

I am light.

I will not be deceived by false thoughts. I accept the truth of my nature.

All that enters into my imagination is illuminated by the light of my being. I give form to all thoughts when I impress that form with the light of my being.

With the power of my being I am the master of the instrument I call my physical body.

I am master of the direction in which I orient my attention.

I command the formation of my experiences with application of my mental faculties.

I release my attention from all deceptive thoughts.

I revoke all power of being from false thought forms. I feel the lightness of my being.

Prattle - Wisdom

Every word I say has value.

Every word I say improves my environment.

Every word that comes from the power of my being and leaves my mouth is restorative, helpful, and constructive.

I use words to build new worlds where all can freely express the truth that unites all.

I observe with unconditioned awareness.

I intuitively understand all parties, their actions, and the meaning of their words.

I am intelligent self-awareness. I am understanding, intelligent, wise, and discerning. I express the power of my being to pierce illusions.

I see clearly. I know instantly. I resolve all conflicts. I decipher correctly. I organize my thoughts and my mental environment. I productively bring intelligent thought that flows progress in any direction that I direct my attention.

I use words to build constructive thoughts and actions.

The thoughts and ideas I bring into attention are illuminating and clarifying. The thoughts I animate create peace between all parties, uniting in singular awareness of the truth that we are all distinct self-aware parts of the one-mind.

My words unite.

I speak wisdom. I think wisdom. I act wisely.

My words unite my unseen, inner world of senses with the outer world of form.

Pressure - Unobstructed

I am an unobstructed channel of creative power. I move any obstruction in my presence. Nothing that is unacceptable to me dwells in my presence of mind.

I dismiss all false thoughtforms born from a false belief of an external power.

The power of my being is the only operative power that gives life to those thoughts that I focus my attention on.

I remove all obstructions in my mind. I remove all false thoughtforms from the scope of my attention. I release all thoughts inconsistent with perfection.

I give of myself only to that which I deem acceptable to me.

I give to myself in the outerworld all good that enters into my imagination. Thus, I am unaware of anything unlike truth.

With perfect understanding, I shape my mind with all that is good and thus the events that form my experience in my world are good.

All that is my good comes to my mind, through the instrument I call my physical body, and into my outer experience. I release and let go of all obstructions in my physical body.

I release and let go of all obstructions counter to the free flowing presence of being. My attention goes into the direction of the one-mind. The one-mind flows freely through me, rejuvenating the arrangement of my mind and renews my self-conception.

Every part of me is free-flowing and I free myself to enter into new realms of truth.

I open my attention to receive a higher understanding of truth. I leave behind undesirable thoughts in favor of new, desirable thoughts.

Prideful - Encouraging

All are capable of the great works contained in the shared connection of the one mind.

All are inherently capable with the power to create, to construct imaginatively, to sense with their mental faculties, and to organize patterns in the temple of one's inner world.

I always remember the singular, fundamental connection we all share and the endowment that permits us to create our own experience.

I sense the enthusiasm of shared progress.

I sense the appreciation of infinite diversity of expression.

I sense the inherent value in all.

I sense the unlimited capabilities in all.

I sense the completion, stability, harmony, and strength shared in one-mind.

There is no competition in one-mind. All rise together in one-mind.

All works to know its true nature in one-mind.

I feel a permanent connection in one-mind.

I feel an unending sense of unity in the power of my being and the power of my being always finds all parties.

Punish - Reward

All upon which I touch and feel with the power of my being with acceptance of its reality bears fruit in my experience.

All patterns of thought upon which I impress into the temple of my inner mind contain their plan of expression by which I bring to completion in my outer world.

I see the logical end of all patterns of expression.

I sense the solution to all false thought patterns immediately.

I correct all false thought patterns with correct thinking.

I recognize and immediately understand all patterns when they are presented to my awareness.

All that is my good is guaranteed to me in one-mind.

All that is my good is designed with me in mind. All that is my good is available immediately to me the moment upon which I accept my good and enter into oneness with it.

The naturalness of my being emanates the fruit of the vine to which I am forever connected in one-mind: joy, peace, affluent perfection, organization, and greatness.

The freedom of being bears the reward of experiencing oneself as one is intended.

R
Refuse - Desire

I accept all that is my good. I accept my true nature.

I enter into oneness with all that is perfectly designed in one-mind. I experience all the grandeur, beauty, and excellence available to me in oneness.

I receive in the fullness of recognition all that is my good.

I allow myself to enter into all the places that are available for me to enjoy and explore.

I allow myself to encounter all who are ready to interact with me in oneness.

I am aware of my worthiness, my readiness, and my openness to my good.

I am drawn to that which facilitates the fullness of my power of being.

I am at rest within the presence of my being. I am steadily oriented upon the feeling of oneness that is available to all.

I release all mental tension that would restrict my attention from fully enjoying the experience of all good.

Refused - Provided

I am provided by the origin of all creation.

I am endowed with all I require to exist.

I was born with the elements required for my growth. I contain all that is required to express and I am one with the origin of all life.

I lack for nothing because I am provided by the origin of all abundance. I need nothing because the origin of all endowed me with the falculties to express my mental activity into expression.

No one outside of me controls my access to the origin of all thought. No one outside of me limits my access to the power that I use to experience all that is acceptable to me. No one thinks for me because I think for myself and I think only of acceptable thoughts.

My desired moods contain the instructions for their fulfillment. My dreams inherently contain the resources required for their fulfillment. My imagination provides me with the ideas for the expression of my mental creations. I create as I speak. Nobody can create for me.

There is nothing and nobody that separates me from my good. I do not need to seek an appeal to external individuals or organizations.

I enter into my good through my imagination and send the power of my being forth into my experience to materialize and come together in perfect ways.

All that I desire to experience is first a thought. My acceptance of this thought gives it expression. Expression results from the engagement of my inner mental activities through imaginal acts that I construct. I send forth this thought into the world of expression and I know when it is done. The completion of this event alters the structure of my world. Altering the arrangement of my mind alters the arrangement of the structure of my world. I, being one with the one-mind, am whole. When I transform the total arrangement of my mind, my world transforms to match my inner, mental reality. Events immediately unfold to reveal this mental transformation for me. Experiences affirm my inner change. I provide the source of all transformation through the activation of my power of being. Experiences reflect this fact.

I provide myself all that I desire first in imaginal acts and then experience the fulfillment of this constructed event immediately.

I provide to myself everything I desire. Everything I desire is good.

The power of my being never refuses me and only gives me that which I believe is possible for the power of my being to give me.

The power of my being gives me all good things.

Regret - Finished

Each experience renders the passing of a thought.

I remain intact, whole, and complete through every experience.

I leave behind false thoughts with ease. I dissolve misunderstanding with truth.

My attention remains open to higher truths. I close my attention to deceptive thinking.

I remain surrounded by the embrace of oneness. I eternally remain connected to the origin of all understanding.

Each experience reveals the expression of a mood.

The experiences I witness reveal the quality of thoughts from the mood generated by its core assumption.

Experiences do not indicate to me who or what I am. Experiences do not indicate to me who or what anyone is.

The power of my being can never be reduced, decimated, destroyed, weakened, or rendered inert by an experience.

I fill and animate every experience and interaction with the power of my being.

My experiences reveal to me what I assume is true about my nature.

More and more with every passing experience, I gain an ever greater understanding of my true nature.

I revise previous experiences in my imagination. In my imagination, I correct what appears incorrect. In my imagination, I make true what appears false. In my imagination, I purify what appears impure. In my imagination, I perfect what appears imperfect.

Reject - Include

I know my place in one-mind. I know that I am part and parcel of the one-mind.

I am endowed with the intelligence and creativity of the origin. I am in perfect harmony with the totality of perfection.

I am known in one-mind. I am distinguished, appreciated, recognized, and esteemed in the fullness of sensation.

I am granted a place in every experience.

I am appointed to experience the fullness of expression in oneness.

I belong to the one-mind for I am part and parcel of oneness.

There is no otherness. There is no outside.

There is only wholeness, oneness, unity, totality, everlasting connection to the one-mind. I am inside the oneness of all. I am included even when circumstances and conditions would attempt to convince me to accept division.

There is no separation. I am included in all that is my good. I am included in all that is good. I am valuable, important, essential, and I participate in all that expresses my good.

I am always directed to experience all that is my good and the fullness of expression of my true nature.

I am connected to the perfection contained within the one-mind. I feel the perfection within the power of my being and touch it in full sensing capacity.

Relinquish - Acquire

I acquire higher forms of thought continually without end.

My attention is open to higher forms of truth and I am ready to express them into my experience.

I recognize and realize greatness in all forms.

In my imagination I perceive with my sensing faculties all forms of perfection.

I acquire and integrate into my world beautiful forms of infinite diversity. I experience beauty, organization, harmony, and order of ever increasing greatness.

My attention is attuned to the origin of all beauty. I feel my connection and my own beauty as I am part and parcel of all beauty.

My outer world reflects my inner world of experience. Therefore, I build within my inner world beautiful thoughtforms that are pleasing and acceptable to me.

I cast out all disorganized thought, all false and deceptive thoughtforms, and I release my attention from all incorrect use of my mental faculties.

I acquire attractive forms because I am attractive. I am beautiful and like begets like.

All that I acquire matches my self-perception. I am esteemed, dignified, organized, simple, elegant, and wholesome.

All that is expressed in my outer world of experience reflects the essence of my being.

Perfect thoughts are mine to experience.

Repel - Appoint

Experiences are simple for me because they are appointed by the power of my mind. The process by which I appoint the fulfillment of my imaginal designs is simple. I appoint my power of being to fulfill. I get the results I imagine. I always get the results I imagine.

There are no limits in my mind. I easily and effortlessly go into each experience with capacity of mind. I do exactly what is required intuitively and immediately. I am aware of the process as it is occurring. I understand the process of unfolding my mental creations into visible expressions through appointing the power of my being to do the work through me.

My outer world reflects my inner world of feeling. I speak into experience only that which I decide is acceptable to me. Everything I have is mine because I first gave it to myself in imagination.

My outer world reflects to me my state of inner dwelling.

My mental experiences flow out of my inner world and into my outer world.

Every interaction is appointed by the origin of cooperation. Every self-aware part of the whole collaborates with me through the connection shared in oneness. Together, we collaborate to fulfill a multitude of imaginal creations.

I appoint the power of my being to gather the materials of creation into a form and structure that matches my mental arrangement. I appoint the power of my being to arrive on time to the destinations of my choice. The power of my being appoints those who are in harmony with my imaginal designs to cooperate with me in unison for the fulfillment of good.

I appoint myself to fulfill the expression of oneness into beautiful, truthful expressions. I appoint myself to accomplish ever higher experiences. Each thought is an experience that I appoint myself to animate. My good is appointed by the infinite power in me for me and can never be taken from me.

Whatever I hold in my mind and appoint my power to reserves for me and repels all else. I am confident that what is appointed for me enters into my experience on time.

Repressed - Expanded

My mind does not think like it used to think.

My attention is free from old, false erroneous assumptions. I recall past experiences and all parties clearly and with perfect understanding.

I do not behave in old ways. I behave in new ways because I have new thoughts and understanding. The arrangement of my mind reflects growing, evolving, and increasing understanding of my true nature. The person who I thought I was is not who I am in truth.

I am free from all old habits and limited thought processes. I think anew each day. I live anew each day. I am free from old mental conceptions. I liberate my attention from all mental obstructions.

My experiences are expanded because my mind is expanded. I reach new vistas and I do new activities each day.

I am not my mind, nor am I the arrangement of my mind.

I am part and parcel of the one-mind, the great, intelligent, creative power of being. I am growing in understanding of this fact and strengthening my connection to the one-mind.

I enter every new experience with grace, ease, and fascination. I am one with the one-mind and I feel good with every breath.

The capacity of my power of being to imagine and receive good, beautiful thoughts is limitless. The function of my being is to express perfection in diversity of form.

I release tension from the total arrangement of my mind. I release anxious thoughts. I release mental burdens from my mind. I forgive myself and all for false thinking and actions based upon false thinking.

With every new vista I reach in understanding, I recognize an ever more striking, beautiful landscape of perfection. I see brightly, clearly, and with feeling capture the essence of truth in me and express it into my world.

I am tender in how I experience myself and all. I am graceful in how I experience myself and all. I understand how the power of universal being moves through me and all parties to higher vistas of truth. I am free. I am unlimited. I am one. All are one. All is one.

Resist - Grow

My understanding grows at all times.

Every aspect of my experience grows naturally from oneness.

I grow more in understanding of my true nature.

I experience and perceive growth in my world.

I am aware of growth occurring ceaselessly in my experience in the fullness of each complete, accomplished state of being.

I am accomplished. Each moment is accomplished. I am complete. Each moment is complete.

The power of my being pours out of the oneness of mind. My power of being enlivens all. I sense the expansiveness of my natural state of being.

I feel the joy that growth brings into my experience.

Resisted - Obeyed

I am one. The power of my being obeys my commands. No aspect of the total arrangement of my mind resists or refuses to complete the task I have directed the power of my being to fulfill.

I send forth the power of my being to feel for and touch that which I direct it to contact. Every part of me is in harmony with the task I set forth to do.

I do all things with the endowment granted to me by the indomitable power of the my being. There is no endeavor too great or too grand for me.

I conquer all goals. I conquer all obstacles of mind. I command all mental shadows to disperse at my command. I will not be trapped by false thinking. I will not be held captive by false feelings. I am greater, stronger, and more powerful than any false thought.

I command all false thoughts and false feelings to leave my entire awareness immediately.

I starve false thoughts by lifting my attention to pure truth. I turn my attention away from deceptive illusions and false thoughtforms. I move my attention to new places that are available to me. I go to new places in the higher realms of truth. I leave behind, permanently abandoning all deceptive thoughtforms. I move the presence of my being to new, free states of awareness.

I, together with the one-mind, decide to grow in understanding. I, together with the one-mind, expand and evolve my understanding to correspond to new patterns of thought. I, together with the all transcending power of the one-mind, endeavor to complete new ways of being and action in the fulfillment of new, original experiences.

There is nothing in my world that blocks the direction of my attention.

There is nothing in my world that contradicts the fulfillment of truth. There is nothing in my world that can stop the fulfillment of truth through me

With the entire backing of the one-mind through everyone and in everything that exists I succeed in the fulfillment and expression of wholeness and completion. Every perfect thought seeks fulfillment through me. I give every perfect thought expression.

Rigid - Loose

My attention is loose. The power of my being flows in a uniform pattern. The power of my being flows from the origin of all intelligent energy through my mind and gives form to concepts that develop into experience.

I expand past all limitations, false assumptions, and deceptive thoughtforms. My psychological experience is serene, calm, and placid. My thoughts are stable and expand my understanding. I build upon truth to create greater avenues of expression into my experience.

I loosen my attention from memories that trapped my attention. I loosen my attention from deceptive thinking and habits. I loosen my attention to enter into new thoughts aligned with the origin of good.

I loosen my attention from false attachments and join with the thoughtstream of truthful concepts. From this place of truth, I experience understanding that generates an action of fulfillment of truth.

I loosen my attention to enter into new realms of experience of even greater good. I release memories from my attention to receive new, creative experiences. The power of my being gives life and expression to truth adding even more beauty, peace, and harmony to my outer world.

Rushed - Savor

When I savor life, my thinking slows down. I move gently, casually, and comfortably. I taste life in its fullness, taking each bite mindfully. I enjoy every touch and every feeling.

When I savor, I feel the fullness of experience. The goodness of life and its wonders rushes through me.

I enjoy experiences with ease and simplicity. My movements are graceful. I am in no hurry to experience it. I take each moment, each day at a time. Today is my day. Today is my moment. I savor every day of my life.

I notice all of the wonderful details of this moment so that I can re-experience it in the storehouses of my imagination. When I savor my life, I pay no mind to alternate realities because I go mindfully from one moment to another.

My breath is easy, deep, and comforting. The instrument I call my physical body is loose and flexible. The warmth of my presence soothes my nerves. Everything I touch feels enjoyable to me. Everything I hear is harmonious.

As I save, I feel supported by and connected to all.

Everyone helps me. My world is designed to help me feel as fulfilled as I expect to feel.

I exist in a harmony of beauty, peace, and fulfillment. The music in the power of my being fills my mind and animates my physical body. I let go of every desire inconsistent with perfect stillness.

When I savor, my attention is directed to the sensations emanating from my presence.

S
Sabotage - Partnership

I am the master of my mental faculties. I choose what I believe. I choose where I orient my attention. I choose decisively to orient my attention to the one-mind and to be guided by principals of truth at all times.

I regain mastery of the power of my being by aligning my entire mental arrangement with truth. I cut off the supply of the power of my being from false thoughts.

The total arrangement of my mind is in agreement with the one-mind. I repeat: the total arrangement of my mind is in agreement with the one-mind.

The total arrangement of my mind is aligned with the source of truth. Every aspect of my total mental arrangement behaves in consistency with truth at all times.

The total arrangement of my mind is in partnership with the one-mind and engages in the fulfillment of truth at all times. I command the total arrangement of my mind to only accept thoughts of truth and to act on feelings sourced in truth.

I command the total arrangement of my mind to reject all false thoughtforms permanently and continuously while I am asleep and while I am awake. I command the total arrangement of my mind to ignore false thought forms and deny them attention at all times.

I command the total arrangement of my mind to receive only messages of truth, messages of love, and to always hear the voice of the one-mind. I command the total arrangement of my mind to obey the instructions of the one-mind and to fulfill the completion of my good.

False thoughtforms have no supremacy over me. False thoughtforms have no control over the power of my being.

I may never again be wrongfully manipulated, abused, deceived, and sabotaged by false thinking and false images.

I deny all deceptions access to the temple of my inner world of feeling. I close my mind from all deception and thoughts of sabotage. I command the total arrangement of my mind to only use the power of my being for acts of love.

No external power that separates me in experience from the power of my being. No other mind that can sever the connection I feel with the one-mind. There is no mood that can separate me from the love, voice, and presence of the one-mind.

Now and forever more my attention is totally attuned to the presence and power of the one-mind alive in me.

I cannot be deceived for the only voice I hear in my mind is the one-mind. The power of my being pierces all illusions immediately and entirely. The power of my being watches over me and over all of my affairs and guards me from wretchedness. The power of my being is always engaged and actively building my good on my behalf. I feel the activity of the one-mind at work in my life. I see it, sense it, and speak affirmatively on this fact.

The power of my being goes before me to touch my good and through this connection I am aware of my good at all times. Nothing in all of creation can separate me from my good. Nothing in all of creation stops my good from coming into my experience. Nothing in all of creation thwarts my progress, growth, and success.

All false thoughtforms created by self-aware parties directed towards me are immediately dissolved for there is no enemy, there is no threat, there is no external power of interference in my world.

In connection with the origin of all experience, I create beautiful, loving, and expansive experiences that fulfill my good at all times.

I use my body-mind correctly in harmony with the one-mind. I feel the goodness and wholeness of the power of my being and harness it for the fulfillment of good in all experiences.

Sad - Settled

The total arrangement of my mind is settled.

I feel at rest within the temple of my inner being.

False and temporary conditions of experience in my outer world do not define how I feel from the depths of my inner world of feeling.

I feel resolved, whole and complete. I feel surrounded by the unifying oneness that is my true state of being.

All is well in my world.

I am calm, centered, and firmly stabled on the foundation of truth.

As higher concepts of truth enter into my awareness, I feel satisfied in the fullness of increased understanding.

Liberation is my nature. Freedom is the manner in which I move my attention freely and without limitation of any kind.

I observe conditions pass in the fullness understanding. I witness events in serenity and calm.

I feel appreciation for all distinct, self-aware parts of the one mind. I feel gratitude for the experiences in which I feel the connection I share with all.

I release all attachment to false memories. I release all attachment to images of individuals at various states of experience.

I see all for who they truly are: distinct self-aware parts of the one-mind - part and parcel of oneness - creative, intelligent awareness - life giving forces.

Save - Divert

I divert resources with great ease. I divert my attention to what brings the greatest value. Thus, I divert the power of my being to animate thoughts that create even more good in my life.

There is nothing to save, only to use, move, and redirect.

I direct my attention to the origin of all which is ever growing and expanding. I receive ever more supply in my experience for my awareness is ever growing stronger of the connection to the one-mind that flows all abundance through me.

Nothing can block or stop good from pouring out of me. I express my true nature all the time, effortlessly, endlessly, and abundantly.

What I create is good, truthful, and beautiful. I am creative intelligence forever expressing that which I am aware of being.

I am good, I am peaceful, I am endowed, I am granted all that is a part of the one-mind.

Nothing is ever lost in my experience. All is diverted for its appropriate use. All forms are changed according to the power that transforms it. All manner of forms enter and exit from my experience according to the use and purpose I set forth for them.

I am secure in my creative abilities. I call forth all manner of forms to enhance my creative experience. I divert and use all manner of forms according to the purpose I command. I move my mind to any state in the one-mind and experience all manner and form of truth.

Scared - Centered

I immovably, unrelentingly center my attention on the power of my being.

I know and accept the truth that the power of my being is the only operative power in my world. There is no external power, no external force that can decide for me where my attention and power goes without my permission.

I remain grounded on the steady, centered foundation stone of my being. I am one with the ever steady, all intelligent and personal power through my intimate, inseparable connection with the one-mind.

I steady and center my attention on the beautiful, secure, surrounding fortress of oneness that is the centering power by which all minds and forms gravitate.

There is no other power, mind, force, or decision maker. I do not absorb anything into my body-mind but life-affirming thoughts. I do not give authority to deception.

I am the final authority over my life experience. I decide what I feel and how I feel.

I am not a victim of circumstance. I am not a coward to false conditions. I am not manipulated by deceptive prattle. I will not suppress the power of my being to confirm my mind to externally created standards.

I am empowered and endowed by the origin and the source of all power to stand firmly in the presence of my own being.

I am unshaken. I am confident. I am stable and secure. I am serene.

I breathe in unison with the giver of breath. My heart beats in synchronization with the pulsation of the power of the one-mind. I am undisturbed, integritous, and peaceful. I walk with steady, centered steps. I am directed only towards my good. I am focused on righteous thinking.

All is well in my experience regardless of external conditions, illusions, and deceptions. All conditions, illusions, and deception disintegrate and fade away from my attention immediately.

Scrambled - Decipher

I decipher all feelings and information that I feel within me.

I organize information into a structure that I understand. I decipher what I hear.

I decipher the sensations felt in the instrument I call my physical body into helpful instructions that reveal corrective thought and re-directions of attention.

I make sense of all I see, hear, feel, and observe.

I use what I experience to gain wisdom that I may apply to the creation of new experiences.

With great ease, attention, and concentration, I restructure the impressions I receive into new forms.

I transform contorted feelings and perfect them in my imagination. I organize disorganized thought patterns. I release all false thoughts from my attention and bring my mind to order with truth. I align my feelings with the origin of truth.

Truths are revealed as a result of deciphering false impressions. My mind is free from illusions and false thoughtforms. I decipher the truth and integrate it into my entire experience.

Separate - One

All is one.

I am a vital part of the unified whole. Through a shared connection, I am aware of my origin and the distinct self-aware parts of the one mind. I access and imagine all thoughts of truth.

The power of my being gives truth a pathway of expression.

I am aware of our oneness. I recognize that each distinct self-aware part is coming into greater awareness of its unity with the one mind.

Unity with all is an inevitable revelation. I am known in one mind. I entered into awareness of thought which gave me knowledge of worlds created by other self-aware parts of mind. I became aware that not only could I observe thought, but I could express my awareness of what I observed through the instrument I call my physical body.

Having mastered the use of my biological instrument, I engage the power of my being in creative endeavors to express designs I form in my imagination. The synchronization of my attention and physical body permits me to create a world that is good and connects me with all.

I rest in completion, perfection, wholeness, and jubilation.

Separated - Inherent

The origin of all experience is inherent in me.

I know who I am.

I experience what I imagine. What I imagine is inherent in me.

I selectively curate thoughts until I create a beautiful imaginal experience. I design my world through my imagination.

My world is inherent in me. I think about only what is acceptable to me. I deny false suggestions. I affirm only that which is true, beautiful, and loving. All that is good is inherent in me.

I see myself as fine. I see myself as superfluent. I see myself as steady. I love who I see in the mirror. I see myself lovingly through the eyes of all. My perception is inherent in me.

I have what is acceptable to me. I savor every experience of my life. I am delighted to experience the expression of my creativity. I feel at ease in every experience. My mood is my experience and I select my moods.

I expand my mental perception daily. I see more and more available to me. I experience greater good and ascend new heights of possibility.

I immediately accept the fruit of my imagination. Only truth lives in my imagination and thus my experiences are truthful. I am expansive, self-existent, and endowed with all the wonder of the storehouses in the origin of all creation. All the wonder of the storehouses in the origin of all creation is inherent in me.

I am directly connected to the origin of all supply. I am inherent to the origin of all supply. There is nothing between me and this all powerful self-fulfilling intelligence. It is who I am. It is good. I am good. I experience good. I experience myself.

Separation - Merge

There is no separation in one-mind.

There is no separation in the reality of oneness.

I merge my attention with that which is acceptable to me.

I merge perfect thoughts into the realm of my inner world and feel with my inner sensations the reality and profundity of perfect patterns of thoughts.

I release my attention from all deceptive thoughts of separation, inequality, division, and external powers.

I can never be separated from the one-mind. I can never be cast out of unity.

I am part and parcel of the one-mind forever part of the oneness of all reality.

All that is good is contained within the power of my being and I may attune my attention and merge into oneness with that which fully expresses that nature of my true being.

I am perfectly expressed in all forms.

I am intact. I am whole. I am complete.

Shamed - Good

I am good. I am not my internal imaginations. I am not the actions of imaginary activity. I am a self-aware part of the whole that is oneness. I can use my power for good or I can misuse it to cause confusion.

Only understanding comes from the one-mind. Confusion comes from a belief in external power and authority. All that is expressed out of this fundamental misunderstanding creates confusion that temporarily attempts to hide, obfuscate, and thwart knowledge of the truth. Truth always dispels confusion when claimed by me.

What I am made up of is goodness, wholeness, and light. I am pure, intelligent awareness growing in personal knowledge of my connection to the origin of all being.

I am good. We are good. I feel the goodness of my being. I release all thoughts inconsistent with the understanding of our fundamental connection to the origin of truth. I am surrounded by good.

The instrument I call my physical body transmits good into my world.

My mind receives good thoughts and creates anew. The power of my being creates a new and uncreates anything unlike truth. The power of my being neutralizes false thoughtforms. The power of my being dispels illusions. The power of my being makes perfect that which was misshapen.

Through an innate connection to the origin of truth, all who are confused find truth.

Shocked - Grounded

My attention is affixed to the truth of my nature.

I am pure power of being always expressing that which I have permitted to enter into the temple of my inner world.

I cannot lie. I only express that which I attune my attention. I only express truthfully that which I have embodied.

I choose which thoughtforms enter into my experience.

I reject false thoughts.

I may accept my true nature or reject my true nature.

I may express subjugation to the external conditions of my outer world. I may express libration.

I release my attention from false thoughts and deceptive conditions. I disengage the power of my being from habits and activities rooted in deceptive thinking.

I turn my feeling faculties towards stillness, quietness, and permanence. I cast away all lies, deceptions, and conclusions drawn from temporary conditions. I remain one with ever present truth and my knowledge of truth increases in every moment.

I am centered and unwavering. I am stable and firm. I am grounded in the power of my presence.

Without my presence there is no now. There is only the presence that is the power of my being. Without oneness there is no now from which experience may unfold. I reclaim my power by turning my attention solely upon feelings of the power of the one-mind.

Shut - Open

I activate the instrument I call my physical body to express my true nature. I express using the faculties of mind.

I create worlds with my imaginative designs made up of thoughts, assumptions, and words given life by my attention.

I open up to express image and movement into my experience. My attention is open and the power of my being expands to fill my world of form. I feel oneness in my world.

All doors are open to me. I enter into the one-mind and experience the bliss, peace, and connectedness that is my true nature.

I open the instrument that I call my physical body to the power and instruction of the origin of self-knowing so that I may fully know my true nature. I express my true nature and experience the freedom, liberty, and light that is forever available to me.

My attention moves in the understanding of my true nature and expresses it through action.

All recognize themselves through me so that they may fully know their true nature.

Together, we recognize our connection and wholeness with the origin of being and delight in this knowledge. Together, in knowing, we create a world where this presence may dwell in shared experience through us all as one.

I open up my attention to receive new ideas, concepts, and understanding. I open up my world to expand to greater dimensions of goodness.

Sick - Fine

The power of my being gives all patterns of thought expression into my outerworld.

The power of my being is whole, complete, perfect, powerful, and creative.

Thus, my only task is to assure that only pure, beautiful, and acceptable thoughts enter into the temple of my inner world.

I reject and release all thoughts of imperfection, dysfunction, disorganization, and destruction from my mind.

I forget all false forms in their entirely. I turn my attention away from deceptive thinking that would have me amplify feelings of division, separation, and otherness in my experience.

There is no other power than the one-mind. There is no external mind other than the one-mind. There is no external influence who can determine for me what I experience.

I alone decide the quality of my experiences. I have sovereignty over my mind, over the direction in which I orient my attention, and the types of thoughts that enter into the temple of my inner world.

I will not be deceived with false thinking. I will not render myself subjugated to false conceptions of division. I will not participate in habits or actions that misuse the power of my being.

I use my mind solely in the fulfillment of truth in my experience. I use the power of my being to express ever higher vistas of truth. I use the instrument that I call my physical body correctly.

I am ever poised. I am ever organized. I am ever unobstructed. I work in perfect partnership with the origin of all perfection to create perfect experiences. I withdraw my consent from all false unions. I withdraw my attention from all limited constructions of thought.

I dissolve all incongruent patterns of thought from the arrangement of my mind. I sense vitality, invigoration, circulation, and movement in my inner world. I touch upon beauty, harmony, and gentleness.

I breathe with effortlessness. I move with flexibility and connectivity. I progress with naturalness. I feel oneness with all.

Sin - Align

Alignment is my natural state of being.

Alignment is the understanding of my eternal connection with all. In alignment, I see truth, feel truth, hear truth, and act in guidance of the truth.

I understand. I am understanding. I am always understanding.

I understand my actions. I understand the conclusionary actions that are informed by premises. I understand the pattern and expression of premises.

I understand thoughtforms that enter into my awareness and can discern their quality.

I understand the reasoning upon which I base my actions. I recognize and can articulate with clarity the quality of my experiences.

In full awareness of the truth of my being, I peirce and dissolve all illusions. I clarify all opaque conditions of mind. The power of my being releases all false thoughtforms held within my mental arrangement.

I feel stable in my power of being. I feel firmly rooted in the connection of the one-mind and thus with all.

In oneness I experience the fullness of my being.

I am present therefore I am endowed with faculties of mind as creative, intelligent power of being.

Sore - Sooth

The origin of gentleness soothes me. My mind is soothed with comforting thoughts.

My physical body is soothed by soft inner feelings. I focus my attention only on the total arrangement of my mind is uniform in structure with oneness.

Each part of my body is soothed by the gentle pulsation of intelligent, self-knowing life.

Every word I speak soothes the mind. Every image I create is soothing. Every concept I articulate provides clarity and profound understanding. Everything makes sense and offers total relief.

I create a soothing environment.

I create a soothing inner environment that generates even more expansive, beautiful, and good imaginative experiences.

I connect to the source of light. The light illuminates my individual awareness with truth.

Truth sets every aspect of my mental arrangement free. I am liberated and bring soothing truths to my experiences.

Squander - Collect

All is collected in oneness.

I collect good things. I know each time I embark on an activity that I am guaranteed a winning result. I am a winner who collects their winnings daily. I collect every prize I choose. I instinctively know exactly what to do to collect the item of my choice. The mood to collect never fails.

Every activity I embark upon results in a successful collection. I cannot fail to collect in any event, big or small. I see myself winning and collecting everyday. I collect everything I choose. I see others congratulating me on my collection. I see happy people handing me my collection.

Everything always works in my favor. I always win. I engage and collect. All I can see is winning and collecting. People want me to collect winnings. The world wants me to collect. I feel the mood of collecting good things all the time. I recognize opportunities to collect. The power of my being does what it takes to collect. I show up and I collect. I hear my name announced inviting me to collect what is mine. My name is called and I collect.

I go places, engage in an act, and collect what is mine. I don't even have to think much about collecting. I just collect what is mine. What is mine seeks me out and finds me.

What I imagine as acceptable to me comes my way through wondrous ways. Wonderful things enter into my world.

The finest things in the world are mine. Wondrous good has my name on it. I see an item that I like and I collect it. There is no secret to my success in collecting my good. I just collect my good all the time. It is my nature to collect my good. I engage in actions that have me collecting. Everybody collects and so do I. When I collect what is mine, everyone wins.

I remember all the times I have collected what is mine and how easy it was. Collecting what is mine comes naturally to me. Collecting what is mine is instinctive. I feel what is mine and collect it. I am the best at collecting what I see in my imagination. I have a mental arrangement that sees what is good and recognizes when it has become an opportunity to act upon in my world.

I see myself getting what I envisioned. I see what is desirable and I receive it through the best possible means.

I am granted what is rightfully mine.

What is mine comes to me because it comes through me.

It does not matter the manner in which desirable experiences are formed in my outer world.

I am a collector and go for perfect experiences and bring them into expression.

I know what I want to experience and see myself coming into meeting with it when I collect it. There is no separation between what I choose to experience and me because it all is in me.

The cause and effect are one. The unfolding of my successful collection is a result of me expressing myself by meeting what I have selected from the origin of all good.

My good is expressed in one-mind. I act with my good in mind. When I do something I get the result I intend to get. I collect my results with open arms and a happy heart.

Stagnate - Flow

The power of my being moves.

I go in any direction upon which I set my attention. Wheretofore I send my attention the power of my being moves. The power of my being goes where my attention goes.

There is no opposing force. There are no obstructions. There are no limitations keeping the power of my being out from where I choose to enter.

In attention and power I go. In imagination, I build. There is no force, no mind that can prevent me from building imaginal designs. There is no inhibitory presence that can stop, slow down, and prevent the fulfillment of my good.

I enter into every new experience with ease and familiarity. I am centered in my being. I feel calm and my actions are directed in the fulfillment of truth.

Events are the merging of distinct mental arrangements coming together for the fulfillment of all intentions. All events are appointed to fulfill the patterns of expression through each party.

I only participate in the fulfillment of goodness. My actions are instructed by perfect patterns of thought that I accept with the power of my being. I cannot fail in the fulfillment of accepted good.

The infinite creative intelligence of the one-mind performs all works through the instrument I call my physical-body and forms my outer world with the thoughts I impress upon the power of my being. This process never fails because the power of my being never fails.

Stressed - Collected

I am connected to my good.

My good is inherent in me. Therefore, my good can never part from me.

I am endowed with goodness. The pleasure of my being unfolds and expresses the goodness that I contain.

There is no division between me and my good. All that is true is part and parcel of the one-mind.

All deceptive thoughts are born from a rejection of my true nature. All deceptive thoughts are perpetuated by a rejection of the truth.

It is the power of my being, in oneness, that is the operant power that animates all forms in my world.

I am connected to the origin of all perfect forms. I may access all perfect forms with my mental faculties. I feel them with my sensing capacities and touch them in my inner world of awareness.

With my imagination, I see and recognize perfect ideas, thoughts, and concepts that bring order, simplicity, and progress in my outerworld.

I turn my attention away from the outer world of experience and turn my attention to my sensing capacities and align my attention with the one-mind.

In this state of wholeness I feel connected to my good and receive immediate knowledge for fulfillment.

I sense order, simplicity, and organization at work and is active within me.

Stuck - Expansive

The power of my being expands my understanding of my true nature and all that is contained in me.

I feel fluid. My attention opens to new horizons and enters into new destinations.

The arrangement of my mind is free from limitation, doubt, and oppression.

My attention moves in a desired, chosen direction with ease, grace, and steadiness. The power of my being is stable, full, and engaged.

The power of my being fills the instrument I call my physical body with oxygen circulating fluids, rejuvenating physical tissues and organs. I receive fresh understanding and wisdom that expands my understanding.

I reach out to and connect with new individuals, forming strong relationships.

Suffer - Peace

I feel the fullness of being. I feel the joy, liberation, expansion, and oneness of my personal connection with the origin of intelligent being.

I feel the completion of all matters. I feel satisfaction pervades the total arrangement of my mind.

I am complete. I am whole. I direct the power of my being to go before me to fulfill my good.

I feel the perfect organization of all matters. I sense the answers to all questions.

I hear perfect wisdom available in me as it emanates from the origin of all truth.

I feel centered in the perfect presence of oneness. I feel settled in my place amongst all in the one-mind.

I recognize the true nature of all who enter into my experience. I am in perfect harmony with all.

I feel the oneness in all. I feel the goodness in all.

There is no division in oneness. There is no separation in oneness. All is available to me. All doors are open to me.

I rest in perfect understanding. I see with perfect clarity. I sense with perfect acuity. I move in perfect form.

I feel peace throughout the entire arrangement of my mind. I see lovely images. I hear comforting voices.

Suffering - Liberated

I am liberated. The total arrangement of my mind is liberated. My attention is liberated. I am liberated from memories that trap my attention. I am liberated from all false moods. I am liberated from all false assumptions and thoughts.

I am liberated from all false thoughtforms. I liberate the power of my being to give expression to truth in my experience. Oneness liberates all from all false assumptions.

I liberate my attention from deceptive thinking. I liberate my mind from false moods.

There is no external power.

There is no external god.

There is no external, separate, divided mind.

There is only one origin.

There is only one mind.

There is only one pathway to the origin of all truth and that is through my attention.

I meet the origin of all truth in my imagination and I merge my attention with it by acceptance. From this source of freedom, I expand my understanding of my power and strengthen my connection to all who enter into my experience.

I enter into even more expansive dimensions of thought. I accomplish greater creative endeavors with a free mind.

My power exceeds all limited thinking, dissolving all illusions and false thoughtforms from my world.

I connect with other distinct self-aware parts of the one mind in the spirit of truth and feel the connection we share in the one mind. We are one.

I feel my completion, perfection, and distinction in the oneness and experience rest, wholeness, and inclusion in the everlasting pulsation of intelligent awareness.

Suffocating - Boundless

I am boundless. I feel expansive and open.

Coolness of breath awakens me as it enters into my boundless body, erecting my posture. I sense an ease of breathing, an open throat and esophagus. Oxygen generously enters into my bloodstream and brain.

My muscles around my neck ease into their correct place.

My diaphragm is stretched and expanded.

My body's organs are in their correct place.

My heart beats at the perfect rhythm with the ceaseless pulse of the one-mind.

Each rib surrounding my lungs rises and falls in a harmonious symphony with each breath. My body is open, expansive, and outstretched.

The power of my being, boundless, is free to go where it wants to go and do what it wants to do. The power of my being goes to who I want to be with as all barriers crumble in my presence.

My attention is free to play and explore any place in oneness that I want to go to. In this mobility I jump, dive, stretch, and revel in the liberating freedom of being.

T

Tense - Supple

I feel the ease of the power of my being.

I feel relaxed, supple and oxygenated.

I am energized intelligence. I feel energized intelligence vitalizing every part of the instrument I call my physical body.

I feel the circulating presence of the one-mind expressed through me. I expand my lungs to experience the fullness of oneness in my experience.

I feel the expanse of my inner world and I project that expansion into my outerworld of experience.

I feel eternally joyful, pure, and unconditioned.

The total arrangement of my mind is clear and thus my body-mind is clear.

The total arrangement of my mind is calm and thus my body-mind is calm.

The total arrangement of my mind is perfectly arranged to reflect the joy of being in all manners of expression.

Tension - Expansion

The total arrangement of my mind is expanding.

My awareness of the connection that unites every distinct self-aware part of the one-mind grows infinitely.

I am never alone. I am never separated. I can only limit my awareness by rejecting the presence of truth. Therefore, my understanding is ever more constantly expanding.

My attention goes beyond all appearances of obstacles and limitations. I am free to go anywhere in mind by directing my attention.

My life grows in all directions. My experiences evolve into ever greater expressions of truth.

The language of my soul expands to articulate higher concepts of truth. My understanding of my true nature and the nature that all share is expanding.

My vision is perfectly clear. I know what to do to clear my mind of false imaginal designs and reset my attention on the existence of my good.

I understand complex concepts with ease of mind. I create resolution to all obscure conditions. I clarify all misunderstandings.

My understanding of my true nature and what I can do with the power of my being through the application of my imaginal faculties is ever increasing.

I expand the use of the instrument I call my physical body by engaging in new movements and activities. I do new things everyday in ever increasing harmony with the one-mind.

Threat - Comforting

All parties in my world are oriented towards oneness.

I intently focus my attention on the fulfillment of peace in my experience.

I sense harmony in my environment.

I dissolve all thoughtforms of external power, separate mind, violence, and disaster.

I turn my attention towards oneness. I direct my mental faculties to the expression of purposeful activity.

I construct good in my world. I create beautiful experiences where all are united in oneness.

I see myself lovingly through the eyes of all. I express comforting oneness to all I encounter in my experience.

I feel collaboration and cooperation through the shared connection to the one-mind.

The origin of all connects all in oneness. I feel the intelligent presence in all and I am connected to the true essence of being that operates through all.

I recognize the good all have to share. I recognize the opportunities to express goodness in my experience for all to enjoy.

I feel the pleasure of being. I feel at ease at all times. I am a comforting presence in my world because I am attuned to the comforting presence of the one-mind in me.

Threatened - Guided

The faculties of my mind are entirely attuned to the feeling of oneness.

I see the path laid before me. I feel the moving, animating power of intelligent presence guiding my actions, decisions, and attention.

I do not accept false powers.

I do not accept false authorities.

I do not accept discouraging thoughts intended to repress my presence and to diminish the light of my being.

I am guided by the inherent intelligence of my power of being.

I enter into oneness with all that is good in my experience.

Illusions fade away in the light of truth.

Deceptive thinking is silenced in the voice of truth.

I hear only wisdom. I feel only excellence.

I move in the confidence of my being. I move in the steadiness of my being.

I glide through all experiences with ease of being and serenity.

I feel perfectly positioned at all times. I feel poised in correct thinking. I am firmly rooted in the unshakeable power of the one-mind.

Throb - Pulse

I feel the intelligent pulsation of the origin of all intelligent power moving through the instrument I call my physical body. This movement reflects the movement of my mind oriented in oneness with all.

I surrender to the intelligent power of my being to recreate my mind in the perfect image of oneness.

My heart beats in perfect unison with the pulsation of the one-mind.

I feel no other presence in me. I feel no other influence.

There is only one intelligent power and it knows me, recognizes me, cares for me, and guides my attention to seek the fullest expression of my true nature as formless, shapeless intelligent creative power.

I rest in the presence of oneness. I feel my connection to all in my presence.

I feel joy experiencing the goodness of my being. I rest in it. I dwell in it.

I appreciate the gift of being. I appreciate the gift of being with all distinct self-aware parts of the one mind to share in the infinite diversity of oneness.

Tight - Flexible

My attention moves in any direction.

The power of my presence goes anywhere the instrument I call my physical body can not go. I am not limited in presence.

The power of my being is infinitely open to explore.

In my imagination, I move my attention in any direction - high, low, far, close, inside, outside, integrated - that I decide to go.

I arrange the total arrangement of my mind to match the perfection of the one-mind.

I do not have to be limited by limited thinking. I do not have to be held back by thoughts that oppose my good.

I expand the total arrangement of my mind with great ease. I explore new places with comfort and grace.

I go ahead into new places in my imagination. I release all distorted memories that prevent me from seeing the truth of my nature.

I use the power of my being to expand the arrangement of my mind to match the expanse of the one-mind.

I turn my attention away from all deceptive thinking, from all false memories, from all constructions of pain and suffering rooted in the rejection of my true nature.

I accept myself and the power of the one-mind that lives and moves through me. I feel good as the circulating presence of oneness moves through the instrument I call my physical body.

I am rejuvenating, vitalizing power of being experiencing the best of all that is available in me.

Tired - Radiating

The instrument I call my physical body radiates with the unending power of my being.

The instrument I call my physical body accomplishes the tasks which my mind endeavors to complete.

I am not my physical body. I am not the structure of my physical body. I am not the pattern of my physical body.

I am the reinvigorating, renewing, revitalizing creative intelligence that animates and uses the physical form as the expression of my mental arrangement.

What I see in my body in the outer world is a direct repression of the arrangement of my mind.

My body-mind is connected in singular thought.

My inner experience is expressed in my outer world of experience.

I attune my attention to perfect patterns. I feel for and touch perfect forms within the one-mind.

I immediately feel the rejuvenating, circulating, and flowing power of my being radiating through the arrangement of my mind to reveal an outer form that corresponds with the renewed arrangement of my mind.

All false thoughtforms disintegrate by perfect patterns of thinking. False growths are dissolved at my steady and firm command.

I maintain and dwell in perfect poise, correct use of my body-mind, and harmonious thoughts attuned to one-mind.

I am well in my being. I am content and centered in the connection I share with all. I am calm, I am serene, I rest.

Torment - Relief

Everything in my world functions perfectly.

All activity in my experience is perfectly organized and is oriented towards the one-mind for the fulfillment of oneness.

I sense the harmony and unity of all activity in all parts of the whole.

I feel progress in all areas of my world. I feel steady and unending fulfillment and pleasure of being.

There is no external sabotaging force in my world. There is only oneness. There is only unity in oneness.

I feel the ease of being permeating throughout my outer world. The power of my presence is circulating throughout the instrument I call my physical body.

I sense the pulsating power of vitality moving throughout my mind-body. My mind-body is perfectly organized to express perfection.

All deceptive growths disappear as I turn my attention to perfection.

All thoughts that used to distract my attention and create emotional distress are forgotten as I redirect the power of my being to amplify patterns of expansion, extension, openness, and absolution in my physical body.

I feel completion and a sense of accomplishment in my world. I attune to the connection I share with all. I feel oneness. I feel peace in all aspects of my life. I feel resolved and well.

Troubled - Tranquil

I am tranquil. I feel tranquility.

The total arrangement of my mind and the instrument I call my physical body is tranquil. I know how to create the sensation and thoughts of tranquility.

I feel harmonious. I feel directed in my movements and in the motions of my power of being. I remember my decisions and fulfill their expression with tranquility. I recognize the expressions of my imaginative designs. I am tranquil in these moments, aware of the unfolding of each imaginative creation.

My imaginative designs are results that I express in the outer world of form.

Experiences are formed tranquilly. I flow in the sea of tranquility of oneness. I merge into experiences with a feeling of harmony. I belong to the one mind.

My breath, physical body, and feelings express tranquility.

In oneness, I am tranquil. I fulfill my creative acts as a tranquil conduit of intelligent power.

I do what is good. I experience what is good. I perpetuate what is good.

Everything I think is pure. Every word I speak is articulated with perfection. Every mood I select is harmonious with the origin of good.

My attention only dwells on the truth. The truth is, at its essential, tranquil. The truth releases all strain, struggle, and conflict to reveal tranquility and harmony.

U
Unaware - Know

The power of my being recognizes truth.

I know the exact ways that my good comes together. Through my imagination, I construct the designs that form the experiences of my life.

I see myself having accomplished that which I set forth to experience.

My sensing faculties are the means by which I know. My inner senses reveal the elements that form my understanding. I piece together inner sensations to form conclusions that expand my conscious awareness.

The designs I form in my imagination shape my experiences. I command the origin of truth to reveal the feeling of knowing through which I may recognize the instructions for their fulfillment.

I know what steps to take. I know which choices to make. I know what manner by which I must fulfill my decisions. The steps are clear in my mind. I know what to do today and I know what to do each day. With every present moment, I know. Knowing is immediately available to me.

Knowing is the perfect summation of input to form conscious recognition of the means of fulfillment.

The means of fulfillment move me to the completion of my intended design. My mind is filled with no other impulses, images, or thoughts save for the knowing by which to complete the expression of my intended creation.

I am the creator of my experiences. The power of my being creates the means and pathways of fulfillment.

I know that I am creating my experiences and I intuitively know the steps to realize my designs. If every experience is an act of my own creation, then I must know what to do to fulfill the creation. The origin of all experiences has placed the instructions for fulfillment within and thus presents to me with direct understanding the awareness and impulse to act.

I always know what I am creating. When I act, I know what I am doing. When I go, I know where I am going. I know why I act. I know why I am thinking what I am thinking. I know the consequences of my actions. I know the fruit of my moods.

I recognize with direct understanding the events unfolding in my experience. I see it and hear it clearly. I feel it strongly.

I know when my design will come to complete expression and I know where I am in its execution. Knowledge is available to me at all stages of completion.

Uncertain - Oneness

Oneness is my natural state of being.

When I am certain, sure, and of definite mind I am aware of my oneness. I am at one with all parties. All are one.

In the state of oneness, I always achieve fulfillment. In oneness, I always feel connected positively to everyone. In oneness, I feel complete, whole, resolved, and perfect.

In the state of oneness, everything works out for me. All outcomes are certain and determined for completion because they are selected and animated by the power of my being.

I move in a manner aligned with my good and on a path of certain completion. I am aware of what is happening, I understand how and why conditions are the way they are and why events are transpiring the way they are.

I am the architect of my experience. I recognize the connection between my imaginal acts and the experiences in my world. I am sure and certain of the creative process and my role at every step.

I know what to do at all times. I know what to think at all times. I know who I am at all times. I know what I have at all times. I know where I am at all times.

I know what I am going to do and when I am going to do it. I know how events will unfold. I know what to pay attention to. I am one with all information and I have the right to know at any time what is happening now and what is to come.

Nothing is hidden or obscured from the power of my being.

All is accessible to me, for all is one *with* me. I am one with *all*.

Unclear - Focused

I am focused. I clearly see and recognize the nuances of the bigger picture. I am bigger than my duties and tasks. The power of my being clearly organizes all aspects of my life.

I recognize the fine details. I never miss a detail because I always identify them. I always spot details and understand the nuances of all situations. Every experience is clear to me. I immediately and intuitively understand what is happening. I recognize all patterns and can change them instantly and easily.

Every life situation is simple. Every task and goal I engage in is simple and I am calm. In every experience, I am given the knowledge, wisdom, and images that clarifies all misunderstandings. I am peaceful and bring peace to all situations. I am the answer to all questions.

I am capable of looking at those things which require my loving attention. I am capable of knowing the perfect solution to all questions and concerns. Every question is an opportunity for me to bring gain and surplus into my experiences.

I see myself clearly. I see myself as the origin of all sees me. Because of this awareness, I know what I am capable of doing and how I can proceed. I understand others clearly. I recognize solutions clearly.

Problems are illusions through which I identify organization and instructions.

I see the environment around me clearly. I see what is happening next because I can clearly see it in my imagination.

I see with the eyes of the origin of all sight. I see the landscape placed before me with clarity, wisdom, and perfect understanding.

Uncomfortable - Graceful

I move naturally and gracefully in my environment.

Everywhere I go, I feel at ease in beautiful simplicity and secure in the power of my being.

I am animated by feelings of poise. I use my mind correctly in the formation of elegant imaginal designs.

I employ the instrument I call my physical body to amplify patterns of rest, freedom, flexibility, and liberation.

I move freely in my mind and relax comfortably in the assuring power of the one-mind that emanates pulsations of serenity in my physical-body.

I am settled and centered upon the truth of my nature. I feel accomplished in the fullness of presence that is the power of my being.

I feel wholeness, oneness, completion and serenity.

My mental arrangement is comforting, clear, and quiet. My world is complete.

I notice the beauty inherent in all. I notice the power and presence in all with appreciation.

I dispel all false words with truth. I dispel all false moods by orienting my attention to the feeling of oneness that pervades all.

I sense my connection to the origin of all perfect motion and allow my imagination to be animated by the creative intelligence that pours through me.

Undervalue - Worth

I feel my own worth. I am aware of my own worth.

I am respected for my inherent value and existence.

I am appreciated for the positivity I express. Exchanges are equal and appropriately reflected in my compensation.

There is no question or doubt to the fee that I accept for my services and the value I provide through them.

I am recognized for more than the cost of my physical labor or time. I am recognized for the impact I make.

I feel worthy. I feel good about myself.

I recognize the value of my natural intelligence, and the skills I have honed over the course of my life. I feel my own worth in such a manner that all of my formal and informal education, wisdom gained from diverse experiences, and unique perspective create value when applied in all manners of expression.

I experience wealth, comfort, and respect according to my own perception of my inherent worth. I give to myself first through imaginal experience and which then manifests through events realized.

I breathe easy, feeling deep confidence in my own worth. My muscles are loose and relaxed. My gaze is soft.

Transactions are smooth and negotiations are simple because all are aware of my worth and the value I express.

Unfinished - Ready

I am always ready to fulfill my nature. Every moment I am present.

I indwell the outer world of experience with the light of the power of my being.

With ease and magnanimity, I am. Present with steadfastness of mind I am.

My eyes see beauty. My imagination constructs wholesome, beautiful designs. My ears form words of comfort.

With my feeling capacity I touch perfect forms. I feel every form of perfection in my body-mind.

I feel the greatness of the power of my being. I feel my connection to the one-mind and the eternal love emanating from me.

The one-mind is the origin of all intellect, creativity, and inspired action. Through this connection we all share, I am ready to express these qualities of being at all times.

Every moment is completely prepared for me. I enter into every experience complete, whole, and capable. I am capable of all good acts for the power of my being activates, instructs, and moves me in their fulfillment.

I am aware of where I am at all times. I know who I am at all times.

I know what I have prepared in imagination when it reveals itself in my outer world.

Ungrounded - Steady

I feel the power of my being. I feel my connection to the one-mind.

The power of my being is steady, unceasing, and everlasting.

I feel comforting waves of calm. I feel centered, gentle pulsations of intelligent light throughout the entirety of my being.

My mind is oriented in harmony with the origin of all. The instrument I call my physical body is stable, steady, and poised.

I use my physical body correctly to express perfect patterns of organization.

I feel for perfect forms with my sensing faculties.

I receive stabilizing impressions within the temple of my inner being and amplify them throughout my physical body.

My mind is unconditioned. I release my attention from the hold of fear.

I harness and cultivate my attention to hold firm on the power of my being. I hold firm on the infinite presence of unity.

I am one with all. I feel the steadying grandeur of oneness.

I am known in one-mind. I am embraced in one-mind.

Unimportant - Regarded

I am part and parcel of the one-mind.

I am intimately known, treasured, appreciated, and held in distinguished distinction in one-mind.

I feel regarded by the power of my being, the origin of all distinction, with appreciation, valor, and great worth.

I recognize the qualities inherent in me that are valuable to all.

I know my worth to the one-mind. I feel capable of expressing my worth at all times and in all experiences.

I express the beauty of my being, the intelligence apparent in me, and the vast creativity granted and available to me to express.

I see myself through the eyes of others with respect. I recognize the purpose of my being.

I express and experience the purpose of my being naturally, ceaseless, with joy and elation.

Unsettled - Structured

The arrangement of my mind is perfectly structured to express the symphony and harmony of the one-mind.

There is no other mind or power to which I adhere the structure of my mental arrangement.

My mental arrangement reflects all beauty, perfection, order, and organization.

The instrument that I call my physical body emanates pulsations of unending power that is patterned after the true nature of my being.

I correctly use my mental faculties for the perfect completion of all that is contained within my true nature.

I align my attention to the one-mind. I stand firm and unified in the power and presence of my being.

I am in touch with the beauty of my nature. I am awakened to my nature and express my true nature in my outer world of experience.

Patterns of stillness, calm, and clarity emanate from within me.

I know who I am. I know what I can do in expression of my true self. I use my mental faculties to accomplish my good: the good that is contained in me that seeks oneness in the fullest experience in the unity of my inner and outer world.

Unstable - Balanced

I feel oneness that unites all.

I feel the power and presence of oneness in me through the connection I share with all.

I feel grounded in the naturalness of my being.

I orient my attention to the origin of all surety. I feel the sureness of my presence pulsating through the instrument I call my physical body. My heart amplifies the pulsation of oneness and the message of truth inherent.

There is no external power. There is no external mind. There is no force in the universe save for the one-mind.

I rest balanced in the perfect harmony of my being.

My mind is restored to its natural state. My mind is cleared of all false constructions of thought. My physical body emanates balance through all communication pathways.

My physical body functions perfectly according to the truth of my natural state of being.

I move in grace, centeredness, and stability. I am firmly organized in the mind of perfection.

I perceive clearly. I see perfectly. I recognize the perfection inherent in me. I employ the endowment of vitality, invigoration, and organization in my experience.

I expect the fulfillment of my good in all manners of expression.

I restore all false and temporary conditions with eternal truth of oneness.

Unvalued - Esteemed

I am esteemed in one-mind. I am known and valued. My individual value is inherent. I am aware of my value in every experience. I am aware of my value as part of the whole.

I am aware of my value. My presence is all that is required of me to express good in my experience. I recognize my importance to the one-mind. I feel the power of my being and this power is of the highest esteem.

I am esteemed in one-mind. I am aware of how esteemed I am. I feel the esteem others hold in themselves for me because all are one and known in one-mind. Oneness is an eternal, unassailable fact regardless of conditions or events observed by mind.

I hold others in high esteem because they, too, are esteemed in oneness.

I understand why the origin of all distinction and unconditional appreciation holds each individual I meet with esteem.

I communicate the qualities that make that all worthy of recognition. I communicate my inherent distinction and, therefore, influence with steady conviction.

I am esteemed and I treat myself and I treat others with respect, care, integrity.

I know why I exist.

I know who I am.

Because of this wisdom, I maintain myself in a position of high esteem.

Unworthy - Important

I am important and known in one-mind.

All parties recognize my presence. I recognize the presence of all parties.

I recognize the inherent value of my being.

I see the value of the power in me and the priceless worth inherent in me.

I am an important part of the one-mind. I am deeply and unconditionally esteemed.

I feel neverending, personal, intimate love in me. Everything that is important to me is important in one-mind. I am treated with respect, deference, and high regard. I see myself as important, indispensable, and valuable.

I create value in my experience. I empower myself with truthful thoughts. I awaken the power of my being when I orient my mind with the origin.

I accomplish all that is important to me. My word accomplishes all that I affirm is true. I accept my good as it is completed in my imagination. I feel the establishment of my good in my life. I know that everything I focus my attention on receives the animating power of my being.

I hear the voice of truth directing my ways. My habits reflect the good I see in my imagination and accept as my reality.

I am free from doubt, worry, and self-condemnation. I expect the materialization of good in my world. I rest in the completion of my good. And I speak affirmatively about the goodness expressed through me and into my world.

I recognize the value I express in my experience. I recognize the resources available to me and know how to use them wisely. I am guided and directed in the fulfillment of my good.

All who are a part of the production of my good enter into my experience at the perfect moment.

Everything works out for me and the world of form conforms to my commands.

I use my words to make empowering, life affirming decisions. All pathways are cleared for me. All doors are open. All means are provided. All comes together for the fulfillment of good in my world.

I am attuned to the intelligent power in me. It is the most important and singular source available to me.

The arrangement of my mind and my attention dwells in the presence of this infinite, unstoppable power of my being.

All is well. All is one.

V
Violate - Respect

My thoughts are constructive thoughts.

I use my imagination to build, to create, and to transform.

I create and transform my experience from one moment to the next in ever greater visions of truth and excellence.

I grow the recognition of my connection to the source of all beauty. I appreciate all forms of beauty. I appreciate the integrity of all expressions of the one-mind.

All interactions are harmonious and glorify the integrity of the power that exists in each distinct, self-aware part of the one-mind.

My mood conditions my experience. I release all false moods from my experience, thereby conditioning my experience with truth. I clear the arrangement of my mind of all false thinking and thoughtforms that would divert my attention from the truth.

I align my attention to the one-mind, the origin of all truth. I embody truth in my experience and recognize my gentle nature. Without effort, I transform all false thoughtforms.

All is one. I am one with all.

The moods I embody affect what I sense.

The moods I accept awaken my attention to my everlasting connection to all.

I recognize my true self in every party I meet. I feel the connection we all share.

I feel the joy, glory, and harmony in oneness. I am only aware of the good available to me. My mind is focused on and directed by truth. My steps are guided by the one-mind. I hear the one-mind and feel the presence of the oneness in myself and others.

Violence - Cherish

I direct the faculties of my mind to express tenderness in my world.

I activate my imagination to dwell upon thoughts of tender affection and construct scenes that indicate the fulfillment of comfort in my world.

I complete all tasks with ease and gentleness. I communicate with empowering words of affirming goodness. I participate in activities with a natural ease of being.

I feel appreciation emanating throughout the instrument I call my physical body. I feel an outpouring of gratitude to experience the infinite diversity of glory available in oneness.

My attention is intently focused upon all that is beautiful, tender, gentle, and serene.

I appreciate the innate genius in all. I appreciate the talent expressed in all. I appreciate the creative intelligence innate in all.

I sense joy and wonder in all experiences. I feel the joy of living that emanates from the power of my being. I adore the power of my being and the intimate understanding of my true nature.

W

Weak - Vitalized

I feel the radiating pleasure of being that empowers me at all times.

I feel lifted, moved, and animated by the eternal, ceaseless, expansive power of being.

I feel the strength of oneness.

Every part of the instrument I call my physical body is unified and in harmony with the one-mind.

I transform all the patterns of the entire arrangement of my mind to match in perfection of oneness that permeates all.

I surrender all burdens that have absorbed my attention.

I surrender all attachments to false assumptions.

I surrender all habits of thought that distract my attention from my good.

My entire body-mind is vitalized with renewing intelligent power of being.

I allow every aspect of my mind to experience an immediate renewal of mood.

I feel excellence of being. I feel the inherent liberation of being.

I feel empowered and experience in my imagination ever greater glories of experience.

Doing good is natural to me. I do all with the power of my being.

Weakness - Connected

I am connected to all.

Through diversity of expression I experience myself in unending forms.

Through infinite expression I feel my wholeness, my perfection, my grandeur, and my beauty.

I appreciate all. I value all. I am uplifted, integrated, and complete in the oneness of being.

Everywhere I go I feel the presence of the one-mind in my experience. I feel the power of my being emanating into my outer world of experience.

I recognize the harmony and cooperation of all organized activity. I recognize how all work together for the fulfillment of my good.

I feel the perfect organization of the instrument I call my physical body. My physical body is the emanation of the arrangement of my mind.

I recognize the expression of my thoughts reflected in my physical body. I hold in my imagination an image of perfect harmony, organization, cooperation, and order.

In perfect simplicity, I move my attention in the direction of the origin of all order. I can sense perfect order in my experience. I feel the harmony in all experience. I feel the goodness of oneness. I feel my goodness and amplify the pattern of organization in all diversity of expression. I am at peace with all because all is one and I am one with all.

Withholding - Given

All is given and provided to me.

Nothing withholds the love and power of the one-mind from me.

There is no party who can stop the fulfillment of my good. There is no patry who can prevent me from using my imagination to create constructive imaginal designs. There is no one who can control my attention and the direction of my power of being.

Perfect forms of all types and manners of expression are immediately available to me now. All I have to do is turn my attention to my imagination and construct an imaginal design that is worthy of experience.

All I have to do is turn my attention to the power in me and direct it to form my good inherent in me.

I desire nothing because I feel my endowment in me. I give myself to all manner of beautiful forms. I give myself all experiences that would express my good in my world.

All doubts, fears, scared feelings depart from me now.

I uproot every false assumption from my mind. I release and clarify my attention from the hold of false thinking.

I step out of limiting and obstructive thinking that formerly imprisoned my attention. I see through all obstacles, walls, delusions, and deceptions and I am directly, imminently focused upon the everlasting, unbendable, and unbroken power that is the truth of the one-mind.

I live and dwell in the oneness. I sense within my being the goodness, gentleness, peace, serenity, harmony, and glory of the power within me.

The power of my being is unlimited, boundaryless, uncontainable intelligent creative awareness.

I set myself free by entering into any place in my imagination.

I am free from doubt. I feel when my good will materialize in my experience. My attention is attuned to the perfect timing of my good. I know when my good will materialize in my world.

I am acutely attuned to the timing of all forms. I am always on time. My good is always on time and given to me.

Wondering - Decided

All of my decisions affirm oneness.

I have decided to experience all forms of good starting immediately and perpetually.

I have decided that only perfect thoughts enter into the temple of my inner being. I have decided to only accept that which is wholesome, correct, and excellent.

Excellent thoughts enter into the temple of my being and I replicate excellence in my outer world.

I decide on all matters of my world. I decide what qualities of thought I experience. I decide the quality of my experiences.

The power of my being provides the means by which I express myself in my experiences.

There is no external mind. There is no external power. There is no external decision maker who decides for me the quality of my experiences.

I decide how I use my imagination. I decide what moods I dwell in. I decide what words I speak. I decide what actions I take.

I decide which thoughts I accept to base my actions on. I decide who I allow to influence my mental environment. I decide what designs I construct in my imagination.

I decide how to recall past experiences. I decide how I feel on a habitual basis. There is no other decision maker in my life.

No party takes away my decision making capacity from me and I alone may use my decision making capacity creatively and intelligently as I am creative intelligence expressing and experiencing itself.

Worry - Rest

I rest.

All is calm in my experience. I am at complete rest while my world is constructed from my imaginal designs.

I place my attention on the details of my imaginal designs. I know the power of my being goes forth to give expression to my imaginal designs.

I rest in the knowledge that what I have imagined is already done and is forming through the power of my being.

There is no effort. There is no strain in oneness. There is only movement of the one-mind.

My mind moves with grace and ease. Just as it is easy to create a desirable mood, it is easy to destroy an undesirable mood.

I create and destroy in my imagination. The instrument I call my physical body performs the work of my mind. My mind seals the instructions of my day's work when I decide how I will feel going forward. This forward momentum of my presence creates for me my mood and it assembles the imaginal images, dialogue, and intuitive motions for the fulfillment of my chosen mood.

From a place of inner stillness, I move my mind to create within my imaginal dimension of being anything good that I choose to experience in the outer realm of experience. I know that upon completion of this mental activity the connections in each self-aware part of the one-mind unite to fulfill its expression in the outer realm of experience. What I do in my mind, I do in my world.

I rest in the knowledge of this fact. I rest in knowing that I create as I speak. The one-mind is the originator of all experiences and they are all finished and complete. My mind simply reaches for what is created and appropriates it in imagination. I rest, knowing it is done through the everlasting, undying connection to the origin of all experience.

Wound - Repair

I see perfect forms in my imagination. Perfection in all forms of expression is available to me now.

I expand my receptive faculties to feel wholesome, complete forms.

I can see the correct form of anything in my mind. I can sense with my sensing faculties complete forms.

All perfect forms are accomplished in one-mind. The power of my being contacts perfect forms and amplifies them through the instrument I call my body.

I can immediately sense the rejuvenating power of my being. I can feel my body-mind reorganizing to reflect the perfect arrangement of my mind.

I turn my attention to forms that are wholesome, functional, and optimal. I dwell on feelings of excellence. I feel the goodness of my being and immediately experience goodness expressing itself.

I am harmonious. I am inherently faultless.

I release all false thoughtforms representing punishment, deception, division, and disorganization. I cast away all forms of disease, disorder, and dysfunction.

I renew my mind with perfect thoughts of expansion, liberation, and calm.

Mood List A-Z

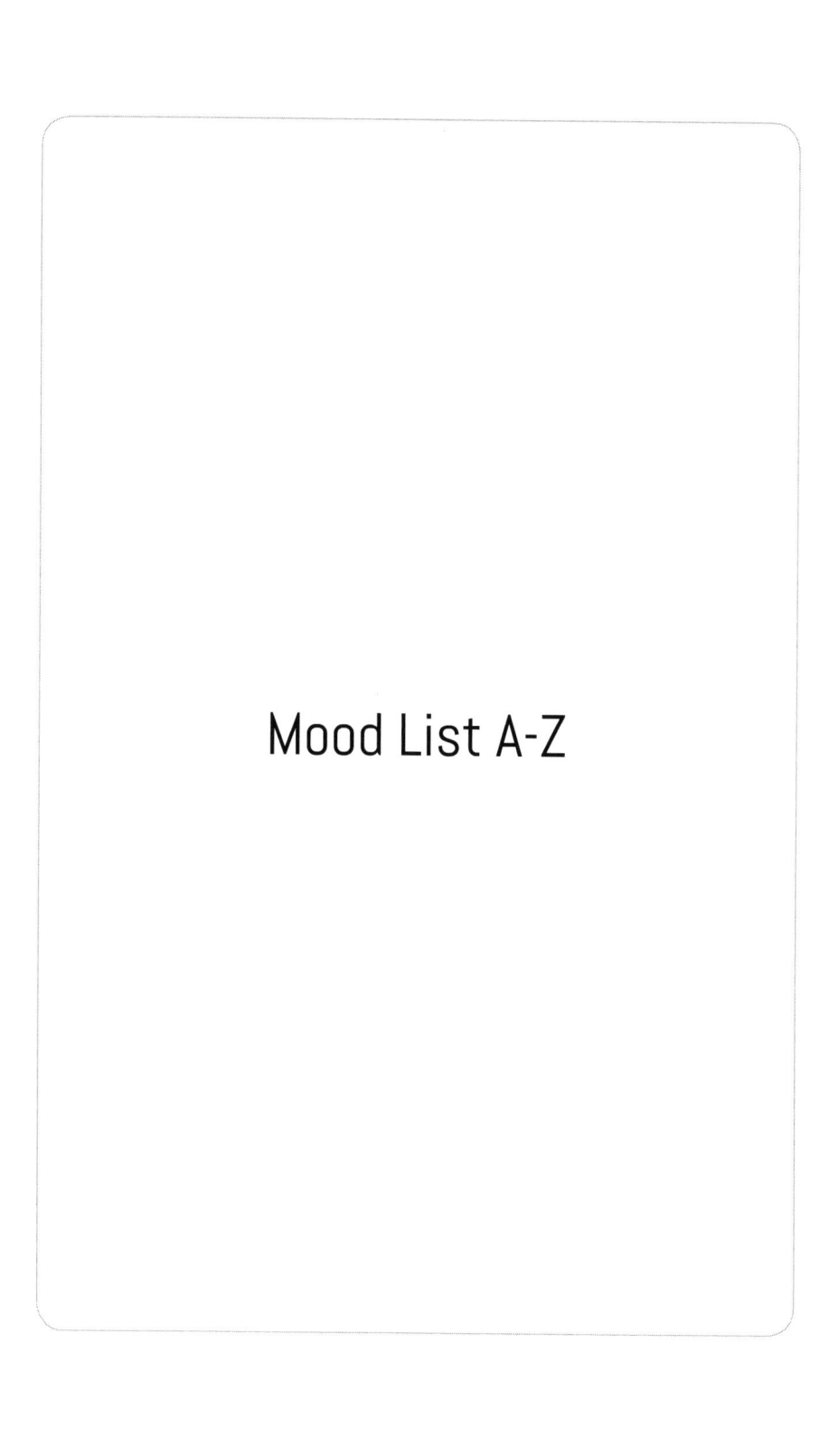

UNDESIRED MOODS FROM A TO Z

Abduction - Absolution
Ache - Soothe
Affected - Cleansed
Aggravate - Alleviate
Aggravated - Relieved
Aggression - Gentle
Agitated - Enjoy
Alone - Together
Anger - Stillness
Anguish - Certainty
Annoying - Fluid
Anxiety - Calm
Apart - United
Argue - Resolve
Arrogant - Equal
Attack - Bless
Avoid - Attend
Bad - Understood
Barriers - Infinite
Behind - On Time
Blame - Mercy
Block - Pump
Bothered - Resolute

Bound - Spread
Burdened - Belong
Burn - Glide
Clench - Open
Complain - Notice
Compression - Extension
Condemn - Appreciate
Conditioned - Unconditioned
Confined - Exhale
Confinement - Liberty
Conflict - Cooperation
Confusion - Simplicity
Contorted - Poise
Control - Trust
Cramp - Flowing
Criticize - Observe
Cry - Communicate
Damaged - Integrity
Danger - Security
Death - Birth
Debt - Enough
Deceived - Discover
Defeated - Victorious

Defend - Unimpeachable
Deferred - Immediate
Deficient - Enumerated
Delirious - Clarified
Delusion - Silence
Denial - Pledge
Deny - Believe
Dependent - Self-Existent
Deplete - Neutral
Deprived - Endowed
Despair - Rejoice
Destroy - Coexist
Destructive - Improving
Detached - Embodied
Difficult - Natural
Disagree - Harmony
Disappointed - Promise
Discouraged - Sure
Disease - Perfection
Disparaged - Distinguished
Dispassionate - Interested
Disregarded - Revered
Distracted - Efficient
Distraught - Unshakeable
Distressed - Collected
Disturbed - Aligned
Dizzy - Stabled
Doubt - Expect
Doubtful - Wield
Drain - Sustained
Drunk - Sympathy
Dysentery - Digest
Dysfunction - Organization
Earn - Granted

Enemy - Self
Error - Correct
Excuses - Solutions
Exasperated - Ease
Exhausted - Restored
Expel - Integrate
Exploit - Empower
Fatigue - Radiant
Fatigued - Energized
Fear - Serene
Fed up - Ready
Fixate - Release
Force - Gravitate
Forget - Recall
Fret - Focus
Frightened - Assured
Frustration - Progress
Furious - Dynamic
Grief - Enveloped
Grip - Space
Grudge - Mercy
Hallucination - Awake
Hard - Moveable
Harm - Restore
Hide - Show
Hopeless - Persist
Hurried - Present
Ignore - Supported
Impatient - Glad
Impotent - Successful
Inactive - Moving
Inadequate - Overflowing
Incapable - Master
Incompatible - Match

Incomplete - Accomplished
Indigestion - Breath
Inferior - Exceptional
Inflexible - Elastic
Injure - Intact
Insanity - Purity
Insecure - Stable
Insolvent - Funded
Insufficient - Superfluent
Insulted - Honored
Interrupt - Connect
Jealousy - Appreciation
Kill - Preserve
Lack - Content
Lament - Triumphant
Limited - Undeniable
Lost - Oriented
Lust - Satisfied
Manipulate - Attract
Murder - Protect
Numb - Sensation
Numbness - Pulsation
Obese - Rejuvenate
Obstruction - Direct
Oppose - Surrender
Oppressed - Great
Oppression - Expansion
Outraged - Firm
Overwhelm - Quiet
Overwhelmed - Magnanimous
Pain - Comfort
Pinch - Fill
Poison - Pristine
Possess - Borrow

Poverty - Fulfillment
Powerless - Light
Prattle - Wisdom
Pressure - Unobstructed
Prideful - Encouraging
Punish - Reward
Refuse - Desire
Refused - Provided
Regret - Finished
Reject - Include
Relinquish - Acquire
Repel - Appoint
Repressed - Expanded
Resist - Grow
Resisted - Obeyed
Rigid - Loose
Rushed - Savor
Sabotage - Partnership
Sad - Settled
Save - Divert
Scared - Centered
Scrambled - Decipher
Separate - One
Separated - Inherent
Separation - Merge
Shamed - Good
Shocked - Grounded
Shut - Open
Sick - Fine
Sin - Align
Sore - Sooth
Squander - Collect
Stagnate - Flow
Stressed - Collected

Stuck - Expansive
Suffer - Peace
Suffering - Liberated
Suffocating - Boundless
Tense - Supple
Tension - Expansion
Threat - Comforting
Threatened - Guided
Throb - Pulse
Tight - Flexible
Tired - Radiating
Torment - Relief
Troubled - Tranquil
Unaware - Know
Uncertain - Oneness
Unclear - Focused
Uncomfortable - Graceful

Undervalue - Worth
Unfinished - Ready
Ungrounded - Steady
Unimportant - Regarded
Unsettled - Structured
Unstable - Balanced
Unvalued - Esteemed
Unworthy - Important
Violate - Respect
Violence - Cherish
Weak - Vitalized
Weakness - Connected
Withholding - Given
Wondering - Decided
Worry - Rest
Wound - Repair

DESIRED MOODS FROM A TO Z

Absolution - Abduction
Accomplished - Incomplete
Acquire - Relinquish
Align - Sin
Aligned - Disturbed
Alleviate - Aggravate
Appoint - Repel
Appreciate - Condemn
Appreciation - Jealousy
Assured - Frightened
Attend - Avoid
Attract - Manipulate
Awake - Hallucination
Balanced - Unstable
Believe - Deny
Belong - Burdened
Birth - Death
Bless - Attack
Borrow - Possess
Boundless - Suffocating
Breath - Indigestion
Calm - Anxiety
Centered - Scared

Certainty - Anguish
Cherish - Violence
Clarified - Delirious
Cleansed - Affected
Coexist - Destroy
Collect - Squander
Collected - Distressed
Collected - Stressed
Comfort - Pain
Comforting - Threat
Communicate - Cry
Connect - Interrupt
Connected - Weakness
Content - Lack
Cooperation - Conflict
Correct - Error
Decided - Wondering
Decipher - Scrambled
Desire - Refuse
Digest - Dysentery
Direct - Obstruction
Discover - Deceived
Distinguished - Disparaged

Divert - Save
Dynamic - Furious
Ease - Exasperated
Efficient - Distracted
Elastic - Inflexible
Embodied - Detached
Empower - Exploit
Encouraging - Prideful
Endowed - Deprived
Energized - Fatigued
Enjoy - Agitated
Enough - Debt
Enumerated - Deficient
Enveloped - Grief
Equal - Arrogant
Esteemed - Unvalued
Exceptional - Inferior
Exhale - Confined
Expanded - Repressed
Expansion - Oppression
Expansion - Tension
Expansive - Stuck
Expect - Doubt
Extension - Compression
Fill - Pinch
Fine - Sick
Finished - Regret
Firm - Outraged
Flexible - Tight
Flow - Stagnate
Flowing - Cramp
Fluid - Annoying
Focus - Fret
Focused - Unclear

Fulfillment - Poverty
Funded - Insolvent
Gentle - Aggression
Given - Withholding
Glad - Impatient
Glide - Burn
Good - Shamed
Graceful - Uncomfortable
Granted - Earn
Gravitate - Force
Great - Oppressed
Grounded - Shocked
Grow - Resist
Guided - Threatened
Harmony - Disagree
Honored - Insulted
Immediate - Deferred
Important - Unworthy
Improving - Destructive
Include - Reject
Infinite - Barriers
Inherent - Separated
Intact - Injure
Integrate - Expel
Integrity - Damaged
Interested - Dispassionate
Know - Unaware
Liberated - Suffering
Liberty - Confinement
Light - Powerless
Loose - Rigid
Magnanimous - Overwhelmed
Master - Incapable
Match - Incompatible

Mercy - Blame
Mercy - Grudge
Merge - Separation
Moveable - Hard
Moving - Inactive
Natural - Difficult
Neutral - Deplete
Notice - Complain
Obeyed - Resisted
Observe - Criticize
On Time - Behind
One - Separate
Oneness - Uncertain
Open - Clench
Open - Shut
Organization - Dysfunction
Oriented - Lost
Overflowing - Inadequate
Partnership - Sabotage
Peace - Suffer
Perfection - Disease
Persist - Hopeless
Pledge - Denial
Poise - Contorted
Present - Hurried
Preserve - Kill
Pristine - Poison
Progress - Frustration
Promise - Disappointed
Protect - Murder
Provided - Refused
Pulsation - Numbness
Pulse - Throb
Pump - Block

Purity - Insanity
Quiet - Overwhelm
Radiant - Fatigue
Radiating - Tired
Ready - Fed up
Ready - Unfinished
Recall - Forget
Regarded - Unimportant
Rejoice - Despair
Rejuvenate - Obese
Release - Fixate
Relief - Torment
Relieved - Aggravated
Repair - Wound
Resolute - Bothered
Resolve - Argue
Respect - Violate
Rest - Worry
Restore - Harm
Restored - Exhausted
Revered - Disregarded
Reward - Punish
Satisfied - Lust
Savor - Rushed
Security - Danger
Self - Enemy
Self-Existent - Dependent
Sensation - Numb
Serene - Fear
Settled - Sad
Show - Hide
Silence - Delusion
Simplicity - Confusion
Solutions - Excuses

Sooth - Sore
Soothe - Ache
Space - Grip
Spread - Bound
Stable - Insecure
Stabled - Dizzy
Steady - Ungrounded
Stillness - Anger
Structured - Unsettled
Successful - Impotent
Superfluent - Insufficient
Supple - Tense
Supported - Ignore
Sure - Discouraged
Surrender - Oppose
Sustained - Drain
Sympathy - Drunk

Together - Alone
Tranquil - Troubled
Triumphant - Lament
Trust - Control
Unconditioned - Conditioned
Undeniable - Limited
Understood - Bad
Unimpeachable - Defend
United - Apart
Unobstructed - Pressure
Unshakeable - Distraught
Victorious - Defeated
Vitalized - Weak
Wield - Doubtful
Wisdom - Prattle
Worth - Undervalue

ABOUT LESLIE JUVIN-ACKER

Leslie Juvin-Acker delights in educating individuals and groups on the power of being and employing mental faculties to experience all forms of happiness. Leslie became a millionaire using the principles found in her book *The Money Formula: Change Your Relationship With Money In 7 Steps And 15 Minutes Or Less* and now teaches individuals from all walks of life to create all manners of abundance in their lives. Leslie is founder and President of Leslie Inc. which provides educational solutions to families and businesses to create happiness at work, in personal finance, and at home. Website: www.leslieinc.org.

Made in the USA
Columbia, SC
26 July 2022